LET'S LEARN ABOUT...
THE SKY

Teacher's Guide
STEAM

K3

Pearson Education Limited
KAO Two, KAO Park, Harlow, Essex, CM17 9NA, England
and Associated Companies around the world.

© Pearson Education Limited 2020

The right of Luciana Pinheiro and Gisele Aga to be identified as author of this Work has been asserted by them in accordance with the Copyright, Designs and Patents Act 1988.

All rights reserved; no part of this publication may be reproduced, stored in a retrieval system, or transmitted in any form or by any means, electronic, mechanical, photocopying, recording, or otherwise without the prior written permission of the Publishers.

First published 2020

ISBN: 978-1-292-33448-6

Set in Mundo Sans
Printed in China (SWTC/01)

Acknowledgements
The publishers and author(s) would like to thank the following people and institutions for their feedback and comments during the development of the material: Marcos Mendonça, Leandra Dias, Viviane Kirmeliene, Rhiannon Ball, Mônica Bicalho and GB Editorial. The publishers would also like to thank all the teachers who contributed to the development of Let's learn about...: Adriano de Paula Souza, Aline Ramos Teixeira Santo, Aline Vitor Rodrigues Pina Pereira, Ana Paula Gomez Montero, Anna Flávia Feitosa Passos, Camila Jarola, Celiane Junker Silva, Edegar França Junior, Fabiana Reis Yoshio, Fernanda de Souza Thomaz, Luana da Silva, Michael Iacovino Luidvinavicius, Munique Dias de Melo, Priscila Rossatti Duval Ferreira Neves, Sandra Ferito, and schools that took part in Construindo Juntos.

Author Acknowledgements
Luciana Pinheiro and Gisele Aga

Image Credit(s):
123RF.com: Mousemd 39; **Pearson Education Ltd:** 5, 7, 9, 21, 23, 25, 27, 29, 31, 33, 37, 41, 43, 47, 51, 53, 55, 57, 59, 61, 63, 65, 71, 71, Debanjan Basak 39; **Shutterstock.com:** Alan Uster 49, Brovko Serhii 69, Bus109 19, Greiss Design 45, Johavel 69, 69, Juli Hansen 39, KittyVector 19, 39, 39, 69, 69, Lynxvector 19, 19, Maike Hildebrandt 69, Mything 39, Newelle 13, 69, Pogorelova Olga 69, Psmans Xyz 69, Studio G 69, Victor Brave 11, 17, 17, 17, 17, 17, 69, 69, 69, 69

Illustration Acknowledgements
Illustrated by Filipe Laurentino and MRS Editorial.

Cover illustration © Filipe Laurentino

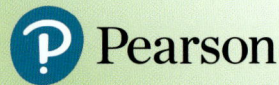

Contents

	Table of contents	4
	Presentation	6
U1	Who do you like to play with?	8
U2	What parts of your body help you feel?	16
U3	Why is your family important to you?	24
U4	What happens to your body when you are hot or cold?	32
U5	Why is it important to take care of our planet?	40
U6	How can you stay healthy?	48
U7	How can you take care of animals?	56
U8	What is your favorite place in town?	64

Table of Contents - STEAM

UNIT	LESSON 1	LESSON 2	LESSON 3	LESSON 4
Unit 1 Who do you like to play with? page 8	• Learn the concepts of *short* and *long* • Make a collage using pieces of string • Identify school items that represent the concepts introduced in the lesson	• Categorize school and classroom items by shapes • Use shape cutouts to build their own castle • Build a tall tower with wooden blocks • Compare and contrast the height of two towers	• Learn the concept of patterns • Learn to identify and continue a pattern • Practice number and color patterns • Create a shape pattern	• Review number patterns • Complete missing parts in a pattern • Present sound patterns • Create a sound pattern and perform it to the class
Unit 2 What parts of your body help you feel? page 16	• Identify items through touch • Review shapes • Build a magnifier to hunt for shapes • Identify and draw shapes from the real world	• Raise awareness of the importance of our hands and fingers • Paint using finger paint • Use adjectives to compare fingerprints and hands	• Remember and define the five senses • Collect nature elements and analyzing their texture • Create a sensory path	• Differentiate the concepts of hot and cold food items • Explore a food tasting experience • Differentiate taste from smell • Build a bar graph
Unit 3 Why is your family important to you? page 24	• Identify and classify family members • Idenfy and share information about live-in family members	• Explore heritage • Draw family members and place them accordingly in a family tree • Build a family tree	• Recognize and categorize actions • Learn and draw a Venn diagram • Categorize, compare, and contrast actions	• Understand the concept of routine • Recall daily activities and put them in chronological order • Build a paper clock
Unit 4 What happens to your body when you are hot or cold? page 32	• Learn to use a search engine • Sort out clothing items • Draw and talk about their favorite kind of beach • Retell a story	• Group animals according to where they live • Learn that some sea animals live on the land, too • Learn about power buttons in technological devices and their colors	• Do a density experiment • Record the results of experiments by drawing and coloring • Learn about the thermodynamics of water	• Understand the concept of shadows • Classify objects into cold and hot

UNIT	LESSON 1	LESSON 2	LESSON 3	LESSON 4
Unit 5 Why is it important to take care of our planet? page 40	• Learn about gravity • Use gravity to create art • Observe how gravity influences the speed and weight of objects when dropped • Use mathematics to count paint splats • Compare shapes and sizes of the paint splats	• Review the concept of gravity • Learn about the concept of air resistance • Make hypotheses about how fast different objects land on the floor • Test hypotheses and come to conclusions	• Compare and contrast man-made garbage and natural residues • Talk about the importance of not throwing garbage on the ground • Learn about different recyclable materials and the color codes used in recycling bins	• Learn about the importance of practicing the three Rs • Understand the impact our trash causes on the environment • Sing a song about the three Rs
Unit 6 How can you stay healthy? page 48	• Learn about the parts of a plant • Learn about what plants need to survive • Categorize vegetables according to the parts of a plant • Understand the importance of eating different vegetables • Plant seeds	• Listen to and understand a story • Order the sequence of events using stickers • Understand the principle of levers • Make a simple lever to lift the enormous turnip	• Understand the difference between processed food and more natural kinds of food • Learn about food processing • Make a food processing machine • Explain the steps to use their food machine	• List and categorize food items in alphabetical order • Create a name acrostic using the food items listed • Present the acrostics to the class in a class soirée
Unit 7 How can you take care of animals? page 56	• Classify animals according to their habitats • Recognize kinds of animals • Classify animals into wild or domestic	• Learn about sequencing and practice it • Identify animals by their characteristics • Place domestic animals in their usual habitat	• Recognize the shapes of different animals • Use a tangram • Identify the needs of an animal	• Recall animal characteristics • Classifying objects • Discuss animal care
Unit 8 What is your favorite place in town? page 64	• Recognize different places in town • Demonstrate a preference toward specific places • Deduce answers based on simple clues	• Infer places from context • Describe places and what they do • Share personal information	• Recognize the importance of different community workers • Incorporate basic math skills into a game • Build a climbing firefighter display	• Recognize different occupations • Role-play as a community worker • Make a paper hat

Presentation

Let's learn about… is a bilingual program that aims to develop a wide variety of skills and subjects. To this end, several additional components ensure that students work on creative learning, pre-coding skills, STEAM lessons, personal, social, and emotional development and much more. Teachers can find a complete mapping of the components online and suggested weekly planning to help them with their lessons in order to make the most of the cross-curricular proposal. All of the components of the program provide students with the opportunity to build a solid foundation and get ready for the challenges ahead.

As part of the ***Let's learn about… Bilingual Program***, the STEAM component aims to encourage students to gather ideas and explore possibilities in order to solve problems and build knowledge from them – and language is the means by which this happens. The acronym STEAM is used to refer to skills related to five learning subjects: Science, Technology, Engineering, Arts, and Math. STEAM skills are mostly developed through hands-on activities that require students to think critically, investigate, make discoveries by trial and error, and reflect on ways to broaden the possibilities of the application of new knowledge.

Learning principles behind STEAM in *Let's learn about…*

The STEAM component in ***Let's learn about… Bilingual Program*** was developed based on the following learning principles:

- Children engage in practical problem-solving from a very early age and they are naturally motivated to do so.
- Children's understanding of the world cannot be imposed; the way they relate the experiences they go through to reality will help them develop their own understanding of the world. Nevertheless, they should be guided in order to find answers and discover new things.
- Although applying certain concepts and skills may seem too challenging for most preschoolers, they are generally capable of developing an understanding of early scientific skills, for instance, if they are provided with visual aid, relatable experiences, and hands-on tasks.
- All STEAM subjects are somehow already part of a child's daily routine: they may identify amounts and shapes in objects or understand that a ball rolls when they kick it, for example.
- Providing preschoolers with meaningful opportunities to develop creative and collaborative work is closely related to how much they may progress in developmental domains and school readiness.
- Students play a leading role in guiding lessons, selecting and reflecting on possible materials they need for a given project, and reflecting on improvements. Although possible outcomes are provided for all tasks involving creating something new, they should be open-ended and support students so that they can cultivate innovative ideas.
- The fundamentals of a lesson include: asking students questions to have them reflect on a problem, plan and create solutions to it, observe and analyze the outcome of this solution and reflect on possible ways to improve it.

What a STEAM lesson involves

As in any other ***Let's learn about…*** component, STEAM lessons propose the establishment of a routine when it comes to the beginning and end of a class, such as greeting their teacher, puppet, and classmates, talking about the schedule for the day, and saying goodbye.

The other activities that are part of a lesson aim not only to present a concept to students, but more importantly, they work towards having students perceive an idea through experimenting. All STEAM subjects explicitly covered in a lesson are displayed at its opening page and in each of the proposed activities. Although subjects are presented separately in each of the activities, all these stages integrate in order to provide opportunities for accomplishing the goals of a lesson.

About the subjects in STEAM

- **Science** – Students are encouraged to make use of the scientific method to experiment and make discoveries about the world. This means that science activities require students to think and create hypotheses before carrying out experiments and evaluating their results.
- **Technology** – Rather than using technological devices as the main tool for technology activities, the program provides an understanding of several man-made objects and basic concepts children should learn in order to understand some fundamental principles of technology, such as common terms, processes, and sequences in programming or dealing with digital tools.
- **Engineering** – When students are invited to build something after analyzing a problem, thinking of the needs, planning and designing a possible solution, they are actually going through steps which are very similar to those an engineer goes through in order to develop a product. The STEAM component also proposes that students analyze their production and think of ways to improve it.
- **Arts** – STEAM is strongly related to thinking critically and creating. When creating something, artistic skills such as painting, drawing, and assembling something in a creative way are necessary. As well as using art as the means to accomplish a goal, students go beyond and explore ways to solve a problem creatively.

- **Math** – This STEAM subject is so present in a child's life that the simple understanding of the space they have available on their desks or tables to put their school material is in fact a math concept they needed to develop. A few other essential concepts that are learned from a very early age are the understanding of sequences, patterns, problem solving, estimating size and weight, and measuring using non-standard tools.

The purposeful integration of these five learning subjects in the lessons aims to promote a wider range of learning opportunities to preschoolers. **Let's learn about...** students should be prepared to combine innovation with taking risks after careful analysis of possible outcomes and engage in experiential learning through problem solving and collaboration.

Components

For teachers

- STEAM Teacher's Guide
- Audio library with songs available at Pearson English Portal

For students

- STEAM Project Book with pages that may be removed

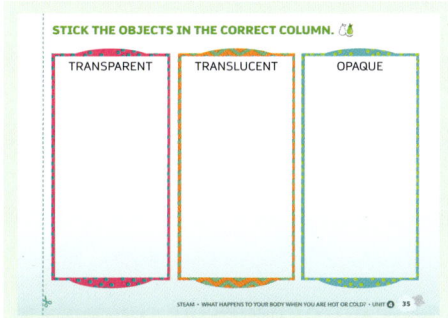
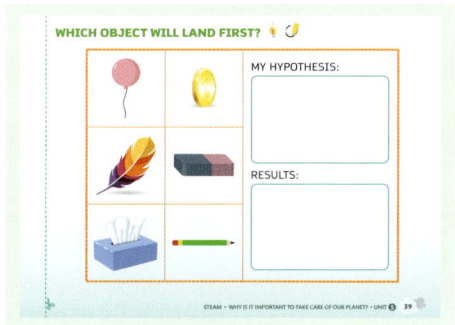

How to work with the STEAM Project Book

All **Let's learn about...** Project Books may have their pages removed. Before starting an activity in their Project Books, students can be instructed to take out the page they are going to work on and add it to a folder of their choice, so that students' work can be shared with parents regularly. This page, together with the projects students have developed in other project lessons, can become part of a portfolio created alongside with the teacher.

The aim of a portfolio is to show the cumulative efforts and progress students have made over time. This is also a great way to evaluate their improvement in all learning areas and the mastery of several skills. Students should be encouraged to share the work in their portfolio with their parents so that they can support their child's learning and be an active part of their development as a student.

An assessment chart is available in the Extra Resources folder at Pearson English Portal for teachers to print and fill out with students' performance and attached to the portfolio folder.

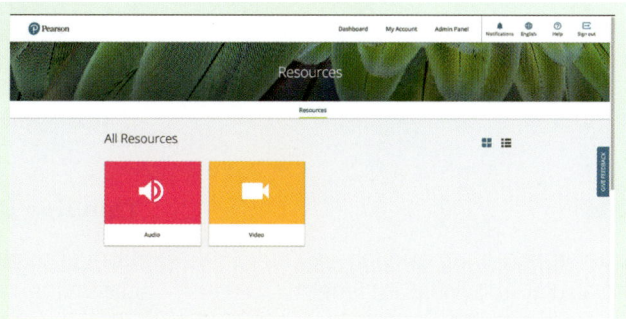

Presentation 7

Unit 1 Who do you like to play with?

**LOOK AND COLOR RAPUNZEL'S HAIR.
HOW LONG IS HER HAIR?**

Learning goals
- Learn the concepts of *short* and *long*
- Learn to use a ruler and measure length
- Listen to, understand, and answer questions about a story
- Make a collage using pieces of string

STEAM subjects
- Arts
- Math

Thinking skills
Conceptualizing, comparing, creating, sorting, classifying

Main language content
Words related to *Rapunzel's* story: castle, prince, princess, sing, stairs, tower, witch
Long hair, short hair

OPENING

Circle time

Materials and preparation
- Visual schedule pictures

Say *hello* to students and invite them to sit in a circle. Show them all the visual schedule pictures and explain what they are for. Say, *These pictures show our schedule for the day. Let's check them out!* Show all pictures, one at a time, and name the subjects. Have students repeat. Then ask them to think of what they could study in those subjects. If necessary, help them by drawing on the board: animals, plants (science), computer, phone (technology), house, ladder (engineering), paintbrushes, pencils (arts), numbers, plus and minus signs (math).

> **Note to teachers**
> You can print out pictures of students doing these activities and use them for the visual schedule.

Math – Comparing length: introducing the concepts of *long* and *short*

Materials and preparation
- Index cards (prepared by you before class, starts with the words *short* and *long* written on each of them)
- Scissors
- String
- Two crayons of the same length

Ask students to keep working in the circle. Place two crayons of the same length in the middle of the circle on the floor. Explain to students they are of equal length. Then cut a string into multiple pieces of different lengths (a 10 cm piece, two 20 cm pieces, and a 30 cm piece). Lay all the pieces on the floor, too. Check if students can identify which ones are the same length. If not, help them. Remove these two pieces from the floor. Place the *short* index card next to the 10 cm piece and the *long* index card next to the 30 cm piece. Point to the lengths of string, say the words twice, and ask students to repeat. Repeat this procedure with other objects in the classroom and elicit from students the concepts of *short* and *long*.

ACTIVE LEARNING

Math – Identifying the length of Rapunzel's hair

Materials and preparation
- *Rapunzel* story for kids (any of your choice – printed or digital version)
- Rulers (20-30 cm long, one per group)

Ask students if they have ever heard of the story of Princess Rapunzel. Invite them to share what they know. Allow them to use L1 at this point. Use the book to tell them the story. Show students the pictures one at a time and tell them the story in a simple way. Go back to a page of the book that shows the main characters and the tower and ask them some comprehension questions to reinforce the new language, such as *castle, long hair, prince, princess, short hair, tower,* and *witch*. Also ask students questions that reinforce colors and shapes.

Show students a ruler and ask them if they know what it is and what it is for. Invite them to say what they see in the rules, such as numbers and lines. Have students come closer to you and the book; use the ruler to measure the length of the tower of the castle and have them help you identify how long the tower illustration is.

Divide students into groups and give each group a ruler. Pass the book around and have groups try to use their ruler to measure Rapunzel's hair length in that scene. Have groups talk to each other and check if they all agree on the length of her hair.

Then ask students individually, *Is your hair long or short?* Elicit from them, *It's short.* or *It's long.*

Note to teachers
A lot of common childhood stories teach basic concepts. The concepts are not always stated within the text, but the illustrations help you teach them. The stories can be used to introduce the concepts, to make students practice the concepts introduced previously, or even as an expansion activity.

Arts and math – Look and color Rapunzel's hair. How long is her hair?

Materials and preparation
- Colored pencils
- Project Book page 5
- Rulers (20-30 cm long, one per pair of student)

Lead students to their desks. Have them open their Project Book to page 5 and look at the pictures. Encourage them to say what they see. Elicit the words *princess, prince, castle, tower,* and *hair*.

Divide students into pairs and give each pair a ruler. Explain that they will place their own ruler where the ruler illustration is now and learn how long Rapunzel's hair is in that picture. Have students help each other and allow pairs to compare their answers. Elicit the length of Rapunzel's hair from a few students by asing, *How long is her hair? What number in the ruler is next to her head?* and see if they all agree on the length.

Repeat the number and use the word centimeters, but don't expect students to answer using this word.

DIFFERENTIATED INSTRUCTION

BELOW LEVEL
Arts and math – Reinforcing the concepts of *short* and *long*: string collage

Materials and preparation
- Glue
- Pieces of string – short and long – one of each per student
- Sheets of paper (one per student)

Give each student a sheet of paper, divided into two columns, and two pieces of string – one short and one long. Ask students to glue the long piece on the left and the short piece on the right.

ABOVE LEVEL

Ask students, *How long is the princess's hair in the beginning of the story?* Write *long* on the board as they say it. Then ask, *How long is her hair at the end of the story?* Write *short* on the board as they say it. Give each student a sheet of paper, divided into two columns, and two pieces of string – one short and one long. Ask them to glue the long piece on the left and the short piece on the right.

CLOSING

Reflecting upon concepts

Materials and preparation
- Students' school objects and personal items

In pairs or groups of three, students analyze and compare the school objects and items they have, using the concepts they have learned in this lesson. Walk around, check everybody's participation, and help them as needed.

Note to teachers
Give students opportunities to use everyday items for categorizing. Shoes (feet) and the palm of their hands, for example, can be used for measuring length.

Saying goodbye

Say *goodbye* to students and have them say *goodbye* to you and to their classmates.

Unit 1

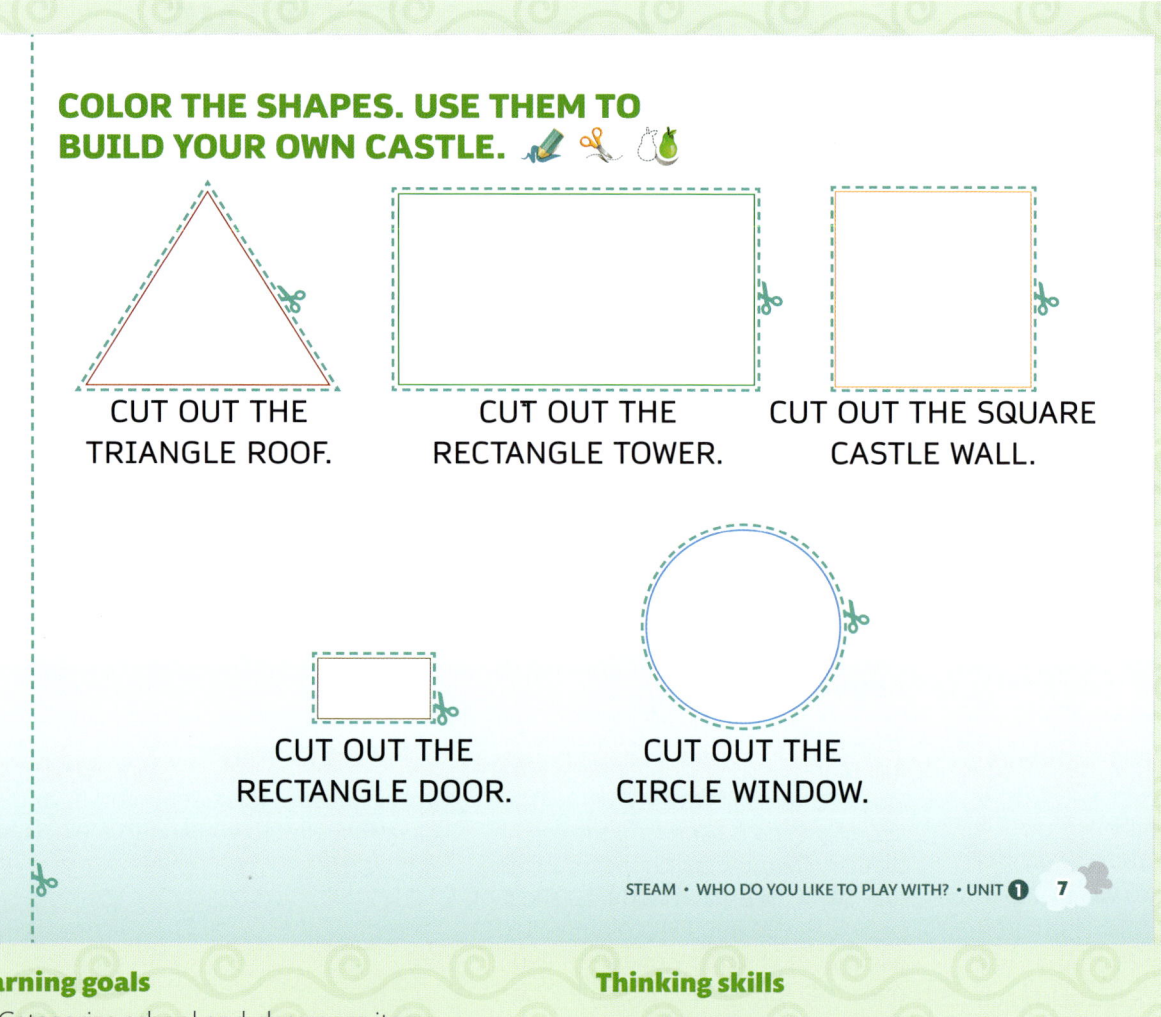

Learning goals
- Categorize school and classroom items by shapes
- Retell a story
- Use shape cutouts to build their own castle
- Build a tall tower with wooden blocks
- Compare and contrast the height of their towers

STEAM subjects
- Engineering
- Arts
- Math

Thinking skills
Categorizing, remembering, creating, comparing, contrasting, counting, analyzing

Main language content
Shapes and blocks: *castle, circle, wooden blocks, rectangle, square, tower, triangle*

OPENING

Circle time

Materials and preparation
- Visual schedule pictures

Say *hello* to students and invite them to sit in a circle. Show them the visual schedule pictures and ask them if they remember what they are for. Have them try to guess what they are going to learn about in today's class. Ask, *Is there (science) in today's class?* And elicit *yes* or *no*. Then tell them if they are right. Repeat with all the pictures.

Math – Reviewing and introducing shapes

Materials and preparation
- Big shapes cut out of different color pieces of cardboard (circle, square, triangle, rectangle)
- Rapunzel short story for kids (any of your choice – printed or digital version)

Prepare the big shapes before class starts. Have students look at the shapes and name the ones they know. Introduce *rectangle*. Say the word and invite students to repeat it. Call on a student to look around the classroom and find an item that can represent one of the big shapes. Ask them to name the shape as they point to the item. Call on another student and ask them to find an item that can represent another big shape. Do this for the four shapes. Show students the story book. Encourage them to tell you what they remember from the story. If students struggle to remember what they read, give them prompts. Emphasize *castle*.

> **Note to teachers**
> Use items in the real-life environment (classroom) to reinforce language.

ACTIVE LEARNING

Engineering, arts, and math – Color the shapes. Use them to build your own castle.

Materials and preparation
- Cardboard paper
- Crayons
- Glue
- Project Book page 7
- Scissors

Lead students to their desks. Have them open their Project Book to page 7 and look at the pictures. Encourage them to name the shapes they see. Explain that they will use these shapes to build their own castle. Elicit from them what part of the castle each shape can be. Read the sentences aloud and make sure students understand them. Allow students some time to color the shapes, then hand each student a piece of cardboard paper. Tell students to cut out the shapes, glue them on the cardboard paper, and build their own castle.

Engineering and math – Building a tall tower

Materials and preparation
- Wooden blocks

Organize students into small groups and ask them to sit on the floor again. Give each group some wooden blocks, make sure every group has the same number of blocks.. Explain that they will use these blocks to build a very tall tower – the tower of their own castle. Have them observe and measure the blocks before they start building the tower. Encourage everybody to participate. Later, allow students some time for comparison and reflection. Have them realize which tower is the tallest, count the blocks that form that tower, and analyze the strategy the group has used to get a tall tower.

DIFFERENTIATED INSTRUCTION

BELOW LEVEL
Math and arts – Sharing my own castle

Materials and preparation
- Students' cutout castle

In pairs, students share their own castle made from their Project Book page and take turns saying sentences such as, *This is a triangle roof.* Walk around, monitor the activity, and help them as needed.

ABOVE LEVEL

In pairs, students share their own castle and take turns asking for details. For example, ask, *What color is the door of the castle? Is it made of wood?* and so on. Encourage students to provide as many details as they can. Walk around, monitor the activity, and help them as needed.

CLOSING

Saying goodbye

Say *goodbye* to each student individually and ask them to say what their favorite part of the class was.

Learning goals
- Learn the concept of pattern
- Learn to identify and continue a pattern
- Practice number and color patterns
- Create a shape pattern

STEAM subjects
- Arts
- Math

Thinking skills
Remembering, conceptualizing, sorting, comparing, creating

Main language content
What is the pattern? Do you see a pattern?
Colors: *blue, green, red, yellow*
Numbers: *1-10*

OPENING

Circle time
Materials and preparation
- Visual schedule pictures

Say *hello* to students and invite them to sit in a circle. Show them the visual schedule pictures and explain what they are for. Say, *These pictures show our schedule for the day. Let's check them out!* Show all pictures, one at a time, and teach students the name of the subjects. Ask them to say what kind of things they may learn in these subjects and help them understand a little more about them.

> **Note to teachers**
> You can also bring a bell and use the rhyme below at the beginning of the class to talk about the schedule.
> **T:** *Can you hear the chime?*
> **S:** *It's (science) time!*
> Ring the bell and ask the questions. Help students answer by showing them the pictures, one at a time.

Math – Number patterns: identifying color patterns
Materials and preparation
- Building blocks in three different colors: red, blue, and yellow

Place the building blocks pieces in the middle of the circle. Ask students, *What are these? Do you like to play with building blocks? What can we make using building blocks? What colors do you see here?* Ask them if they have ever built a building block tower, like the one Rapunzel lives in. Tell students they are going to make patterns using the building blocks pieces. Tell them that a pattern is a sequence that repeats itself: we can make a pattern with colors, numbers, shapes, pictures, noises, and many other things by combining them. Use the pieces to begin different patterns and call on a few students to continue them. After that, ask some students to begin a tower using a pattern and give the tower to a friend, who has to continue it with the same pattern.

Note to teachers

Here are some examples of patterns you can use:
- ABAB (blue/yellow/blue/yellow...)
- ABC (blue/yellow/red, blue/yellow/red,...)
- AABB (blue/blue/red/red, blue/blue/red/red)

ACTIVE LEARNING

Math – Number patterns

Materials and preparation
- Numbers 1-3 written on small index cards – one set for every two students (each set should have three copies of every number)

Tell students they are going to make patterns with numbers. Use one of the sets to make a pattern and ask students to continue the pattern for you (e.g.: 1/1/2, 2/2/3, 3/3/1, etc.).
Call on a student and tell them to begin a pattern; then ask another student to continue the number pattern the first student created. Sit students in pairs and hand out one set of numbers to each pair. Monitor their work as they create patterns and give them to their partners to continue.

Arts and math – Make a pattern for the snake's skin.

Materials and preparation
- Colored pencils
- Project Book page 9

Lead students to their desks. Have them open their Project Book to page 9 and look at the picture. Ask them what they see and ask if they can remember the name of the animal. Ask them to repeat the word *snake* and emphasize the /s/ sound. Explain that they are going to create a beautiful pattern for the snake's skin using different shapes. Show students the shapes around the page and elicit their names. Tell them to make sure they decide on the pattern and that they repeat it correctly along the snake's body. After they draw the pattern, they can choose the colors they want to use and color the skin. Monitor their work and help students below level to create their patterns when needed.

DIFFERENTIATED INSTRUCTION

BELOW LEVEL
Present your patterns.

Students present their snake patterns to the class using, *This is my pattern: (square/square/triangle)*.

ABOVE LEVEL

Students present their snake patterns to the class using, *This is my snake and this is its skin pattern: (blue square/blue square/yellow triangle)*.

CLOSING

Make a pattern bracelet.

Materials and preparation
- Assorted bracelet beads (in different colors and shapes)
- Bracelet rubber (enough for one bracelet per student)

Students use the beads and the bracelet rubber to make a bracelet with a pattern they create. After students finish it, they show their bracelets to the class and explain the pattern they created.

Saying goodbye

Say *goodbye* to students and have them say *goodbye* to you and to their classmates.

Learning goals
- Review number patterns
- Complete missing parts in a pattern
- Learn about sound patterns
- Create a sound pattern and perform it to the class

STEAM subjects
- Arts
- Math

Thinking skills
Remembering, conceptualizing, sorting, comparing, creating

Main language content
What is the pattern? Do you see a pattern? Can you hear the pattern?
Activities: *clap, listen, number, pattern, play, snap, sound, stomp*

OPENING

Circle time

Materials and preparation
- Visual schedule pictures

Say *hello* to students and invite them to sit in a circle. Show them the visual schedule pictures and explain what they are for. Say, *These pictures show our schedule for the day. Let's check them out?* Show all pictures, one at a time, and teach students the name of the subjects. Ask them to say what kind of things they may learn in these subjects and help them understand a little more about them.

> **Note to teachers**
> Call on a student to be the class helper of the day. Tell this student to help you select the pictures that represent what you are doing that day in class.

Math – Reviewing number patterns

Materials and preparation
- Numbers 1-10 from the previous STEAM class (various sets).

Ask students who remembers the last project activity they did (the snake's skin). Ask if they remember how to make a number pattern. Tell them you are going to show them a pattern, but this time, instead of continuing the pattern, they are going to complete its missing parts. Then show students the following pattern and tell them to complete the missing parts:

1, 2, 1, 2 – 3, 4, __, 4
1, 1, 2, 2, 3, 3 – 4, 4, __, __, __, 6
1, 3, 5, __, 9, __, __

Call on different students and ask them to complete the patterns. Invite students above level to make their own number patterns while the others try to complete them.

ACTIVE LEARNING

Coding sounds

Materials and preparation

- Marker
- Video about body percussion TTU Jazz Classes: body percussion by Kris Olson, music by Flynn Cohen, available on YouTube

Tell students if they know that it is possible to make music using our body. Show them the video and tell them that this is called *body percussion*. Tell them they are going to practice a few sounds we can make with our body. Present the words *clap* (by clapping your hands, *stomp* (by stomping your foot, and *snap* (by snapping your fingers). Assign a code to each sound: number 1 for *clap*, number 2 for *stomp*, and number 3 for *snap*. Write the code on the board and practice with them. Tell them you are going to call out a number and they have to make the sound according to the codes. Change patterns and make them progressively more difficult. Allow students some time to figure out the sequence and be able to make the sound pattern with no mistakes.

Arts and math – Make your own song using body sounds.

Materials and preparation

- Project Book page 11

Tell students to go back to their desks and have them open their Project Book to page 11. Tell them that now they are going to compose a song using the body sounds and the patterns they have practiced. Have them look at the code box and use the same code you put on the board for practice. Then they should write the number pattern according to the code and the body sounds they want to use. Their song should have at least four different patterns, which should be described in different lines on the page. Monitor their work as they compose their songs. At the end, they present their songs to the class.

DIFFERENTIATED INSTRUCTION

BELOW LEVEL
Create a new song.

Students make three different sounds. Allow time for them to practice their songs before they perform to the class.

ABOVE LEVEL

Students come up with a different code to their sounds and create a song with six different sounds. They can perform with other students above level, like an "orchestra".

CLOSING

Saying goodbye

Say *goodbye* to each student individually and ask them to say what their favorite part of the class was.

Unit 2 What parts of your body help you feel?

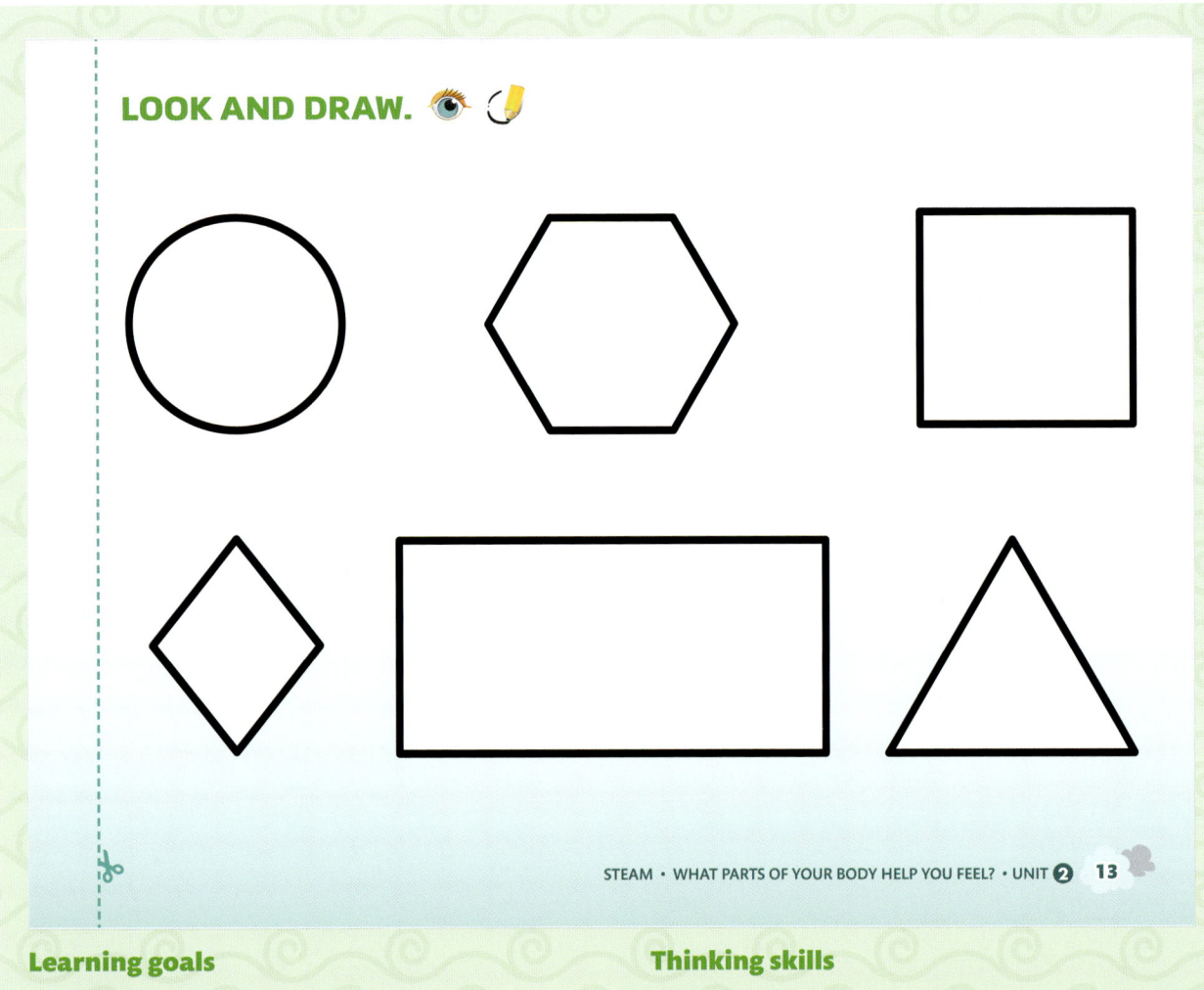

Learning goals
- Identify items through touch
- Review shapes
- Build a magnifier to hunt for shapes
- Identify and draw shapes from the real world

STEAM subjects
- Science
- Arts
- Math

Thinking skills

Remembering, recognizing, making associations, categorizing, memorizing, comparing, analyzing

Main language content

Shapes: *circle, hexagon, rectangle, rhombus, square, triangle*
Adjectives: *long, short*
It's (a triangle) shape. It's (long). It feels like a (pretzel).

OPENING

Circle time

Materials and preparation
- Visual schedule pictures

Say *hello* to students and invite them to sit in a circle. Show them the visual schedule pictures and explain what they are for. Say, *These pictures show our schedule for the day. Let's check them out!* Show all pictures, one at a time, and teach students the name of the subjects. Ask them to say what kind of things they may learn in these subjects and help them understand a little more aboutthem.

> **Note to teachers**
> You can print out pictures of students doing these activities and use them for the visual schedule.

Science – Touch: What do I feel?

Materials and preparation
- Non-transparent bags with the following items in each of them: square sandpaper, wet cotton balls, uncooked pasta, small plastic balls
- Matchboxes

Place all the bags filled with the items in the middle of the circle on the floor (one item per bag). Invite students one at a time to put their hands into the bags in order to feel the items inside. Tell them not to share their thoughts about what they believe the item is until everyone has had their go. After that, put your own hands inside one of the bags, feel the item, and say *It's (a round) shape. It's (long). It feels like (pasta).*

ACTIVE LEARNING

Science and arts – Making a magnifier and hunting for shapes

Materials and preparation

- Black cardstock (or cardboard)
- Glue
- Magnifier template (draw the shape of a magnifying glass on black cardstock before class)
- Markers
- Masking tape
- Plastic bags (or any other strong transparent piece of plastic)
- Scissors

Tell students they are going to build a magnifier to go shape hunting. Before the class, trace the shape of a magnifying glass on black cardstock or cardboard. Hand out the cardboard with the magnifier already traced for students and have them cut it out. Ask them to cut out the middle circle for the lenses, help them if necessary. Have them use this circle as a template to make the lenses out of plastic bags. Help them use a masking tape to stick the plastic circles onto the magnifying glass. Encourage them to play with the magnifying glass by pretending to be detectives and looking for items around the class. Say, *Look for erasers! Look for something green! Look for something small.*

Next, invite students to go on a shape hunt. Elicit the names of the shapes they have seen so far (triangle, hexagon, trapezoid, rectangle, circle, square, rhombus, etc.). Ask them where we usually see each shape. Give them an example, *The signs on the street are circles and rectangles.* Help them with vocabulary. Hand out markers to students and ask them to draw a shape in the center of their magnifier (the plastic lenses). Encourage students to stand up and search for shapes around the classroom using their magnifiers. When they find a shape that looks like that on their magnifier, have them call out *I spy with my little eye a (triangle).* Write the sentence on the board and ask students to repeat. Allow them some time to do the task, then have students exchange magnifiers (since each one has drawn a different shape on their magnifier) to identify different shapes.

Look and draw.

Materials and preparation

- Colored pencils
- Project Book page 13

Lead students to their desks. Have them open their Project Book to page 13 and look at the pictures. Encourage them to say what they see. Elicit the names of the shapes. Invite students to draw in each shape the objects they saw with the magnifiers.

DIFFERENTIATED INSTRUCTION

BELOW LEVEL
Math – Reinforcing the concepts of different shapes

Help students find the shapes around them by connecting the shapes to real objects. Have them say, *Look! A book! It's a rectangle. Look! An eraser! It's a circle.*

ABOVE LEVEL

Have students count the items they have found of each shape and say the number, *Look! A book! It's a rectangle. Look! Two erasers! They're circles.*

CLOSING

Comparing

In pairs or groups of three, students analyze and compare the school items they have in their pencil cases, using the concepts they have learned in this lesson.

Saying goodbye

Say *goodbye* to students and have them say *goodbye* back.

LOOK AND PRINT. HOW DIFFERENT ARE OUR FINGERPRINTS? 👁

LEFT HAND

RIGHT HAND

STEAM • WHAT PARTS OF YOUR BODY HELP YOU FEEL? • UNIT ❷ 15

Learning goals
- Raise awareness of the importance of our hands and fingers
- Paint using finger paint
- Use adjectives to compare fingerprints and hands
- Stamp fingerprints

STEAM subjects
- Science
- Arts
- Math

Thinking skills
Focusing attention, observing, measuring, making comparisons, analyzing, evaluating

Main language content
Activities: *clap, draw, eat, paint, play, write*
I can (eat) with my hands.
Our fingerprints are different/the same.
Look! These are my fingerprints.
My fingerprints are smaller/bigger.

OPENING

Circle time
Materials and preparation
- Visual schedule pictures

Say *hello* to students and invite them to sit in a circle. Show them the visual schedule pictures and explain what they are for. Say, *These pictures show our schedule for the day. Let's check them out!* Show all pictures, one at a time, and teach students the name of the subjects. Ask them to say what kind of things they may learn in these subjects and help them understand a little more about them.

Arts – Getting to know our fingers better
Materials and preparation
- Video and lyrics to the song

Introduce the song *Tommy thumb* to students. Play it for the first time. You sing and do the gestures while students pay attention. Play it again and invite students to do the gestures with you while they listen. Play it for the third time and encourage everybody to do the gestures and sing.

> **Note to teachers**
> **Lyrics**
> *Tommy Thumb,*
> *Tommy Thumb,*
> *Where are you?*
> *Here I am,*
> *Here I am,*
> *How do you do? (or How are you?)*
>
> *Peter Pointer,*
> *Peter Pointer,*
> *Where are you?*
> *Here I am,*
> *Here I am,*
> *How do you do? (or How are you?)*

18 STEAM

Toby Tall,
Toby Tall,
Where are you?
Here I am,
Here I am,
How do you do? (or How are you?)

Ruby Ring,
Ruby Ring,
Where are you?
Here I am,
Here I am,
How do you do? (or How are you?)

Baby Small,
Baby Small,
Where are you?
Here I am,
Here I am,
How do you do? (or How are you?)

The song is available at https://www.nurseryrhymes.org/tommy-thumb-where-are-you.html (accessed on August 27, 2019).

ACTIVE LEARNING

Arts – Finger painting

Materials and preparation
- Audio library - songs
- Cardboard paper
- Finger paint

Ask students what they know about fingerprints. Hand each student a piece of cardboard paper and finger paint and have them make a painting using their fingers. Invite them to sit or lie on the floor. Play a song of students' choice while they are painting. Monitor the activity and ask them how they are feeling. Having finished, have students hand in their paintings and make an exhibit. Invite students to reflect upon everything they do with their hands. Help them say, *I can... with my hands (eat, clap, draw, paint, write, hold and carry things, play games, playing on the computer etc.).*

Science, arts, and math – Look and print. How different are our fingerprints?

Materials and preparation
- Digital camera
- Magnifiers (one for each pair of students or have pairs share)
- Project Book page 15
- Paint
- Washing facilities
- Sheets of paper

Lead students to their desks. Have them open their Project Book to page 15 and look at the images. Have them count how many little boxes there are and encourage them to guess what they will draw inside the boxes. Show students how we can stamp our fingerprints. Introduce the word *fingerprints* and have them repeat. Invite them to stamp their fingerprints on a sheet of paper. Tell students to paint their fingers with a color of their choice. Allow them to experiment many times before actually stamping their fingers inside the little boxes. Explain that they are going to make a fingerprint record and analyze their fingerprints. Invite them to print their fingerprints in the boxes of their fingerprint record in their books. Clarify that each box is for a finger. Have them stamp their right-hand fingerprints on the first line and their left-hand fingerprints on the second line.

Have them wash their hands. Hand magnifiers to students and encourage them to study their fingerprints. Ask them, *What do you see? Are they the same or different*. Have them compare their fingerprints. Introduce the sentences, *Our fingerprints are different.; Our fingerprints are the same.* Write them down on the board for students' reference, have them repeat, and use them when comparing the fingerprints. Use a digital camera to take pictures of the fingerprints records and place it in the students' folders.

Note to teachers
If time allows, you may go further in the topic before you assign the activity. Suggested questions: *Why do you think fingerprints are important? Do we leave fingerprints on everything we touch? Imagine if we didn't have fingerprints.*

DIFFERENTIATED INSTRUCTION

BELOW LEVEL
Show your fingerprints.

Materials and preparation
- Project Book page 15

In pairs, students show each other their fingerprints and say, *Look! These are my fingerprints.*

ABOVE LEVEL

In pairs, students compare their fingerprints and talk about similarities and differences. Encourage them to say, *My fingerprints are smaller. My fingerprints are bigger.* Select two Project Books and model before you assign the task.

CLOSING

Play *Walk, walk, walk... Stop!*

Have students stand up and walk around as you chant *Walk, walk, walk,...* Say *stop* and have them stand in front of another classmate. They will put the palm of one of their hands together with their classmate's and check whose hand is bigger or smaller. Play the game a few more times.

Saying goodbye

Say *goodbye* to each student individually and ask them to say what their favorite part of the class was.

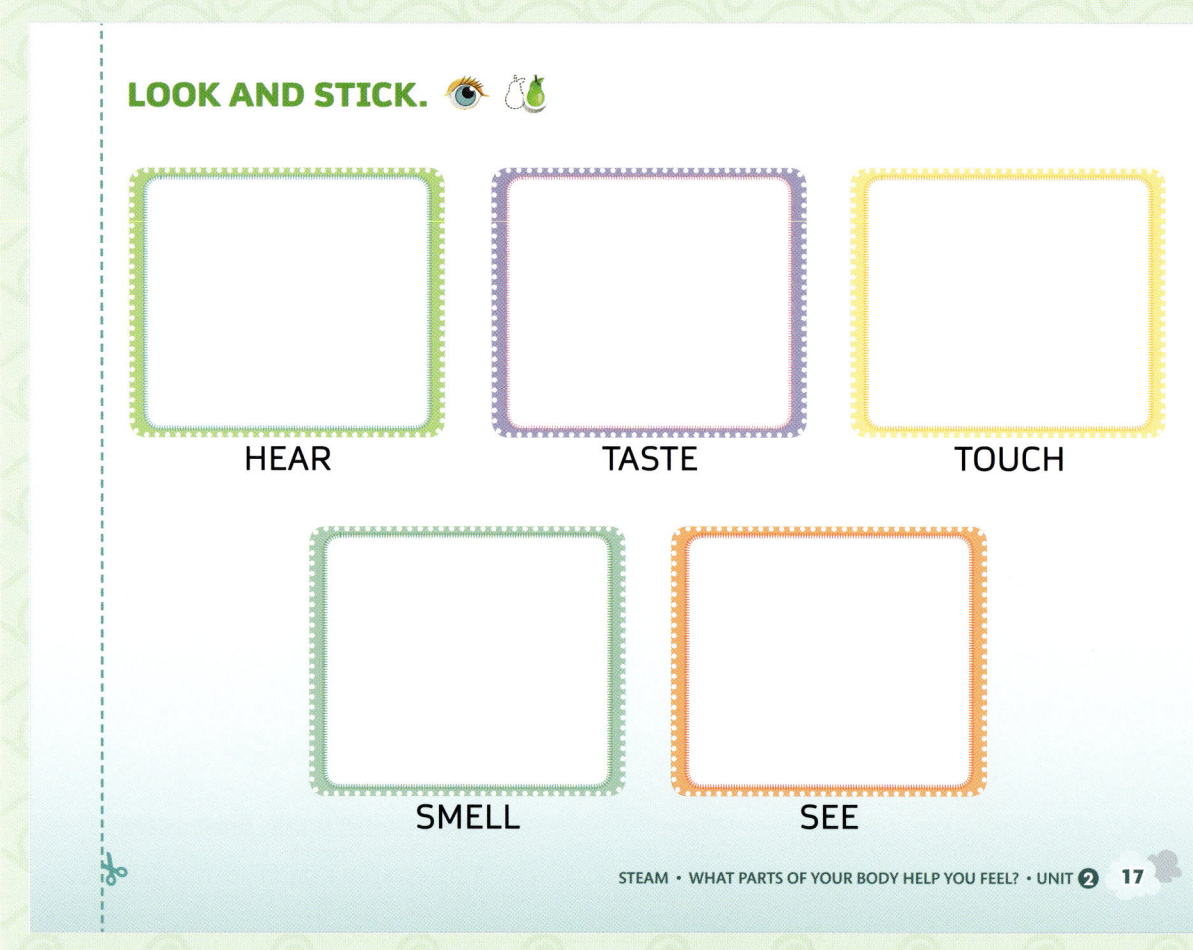

OPENING

Circle time

Materials and preparation
- Visual schedule pictures

Say *hello* to students and invite them to sit in a circle. Show them the visual schedule pictures and explain what they are for. Say, *These pictures show our schedule for the day. Let's check them out!* Show all pictures, one at a time, and teach students the name of the subjects. Ask them to say what kind of things they may learn in these subjects and help them understand a little more about them.

> **Note to teachers**
> You can print out pictures of students doing these activities and use them for the visual schedule.

Science – Checking our senses: A walk outside

Materials and preparation
- Dirt
- Leaves
- Sticks
- Stones

Invite students to take a walk around the school premises. Have them collect leaves, small stones, sticks, and dirt. If taking a walk is not possible, make sure you can provide students with this material. Have them manipulate the material. Encourage students to tell you how they feel by using their senses. Model the sentences for them and encourage them to say: *It is (soft, hard, cold, hot). It smells (good, bad).* Help them with vocabulary, if needed.

> **Note to teachers**
> If there isn't an area in the school where students can do these activities, prepare the material beforehand and place it around the playground area in the school for students to look for them.

Learning goals
- Remembering and defining the five senses
- Collecting nature elements and analyzing their texture
- Creating a sensory path

STEAM subjects
- Science
- Arts

Thinking skills
Exploring, concluding, recognizing, describing

Main language content
It is (soft, hard, cold, hot).
It smells (good, bad).
I feel it soft/hard/hot.
Senses: *hear, see, smell, taste, touch*
Nature: *dirt, leaves, sticks, stones*

STEAM

ACTIVE LEARNING

Science – Sensory path

Materials and preparation
- Butcher paper
- Dirt
- Leaves
- Sticks
- Stones
- Sticky tape

Place the butcher paper on the floor. Make sure you fix it well with sticky tape. Have students spread the leaves, stones, sticks, and dirt on the butcher paper, creating a sensory path. Help students remove their shoes and socks. Invite them to walk on this path, feeling the different textures and the temperature. Have each student walk along the path twice. First, with their eyes closed, ask them to identify what they are stepping on; then repeat with their eyes open. Have students make observations such as, *It feels soft/hard/hot*, etc. Ask students to think about what else they can put on their sensory path. Encourage them to find extra material around the classroom, add it to their path, step on it, and make observations, too.

> **Note to teachers**
> Make sure students are careful so as not to get hurt when stepping on sticks or stones. You can help by holding their leg and having them slightly step on these items.

Science and arts – Look and stick.

Materials and preparation
- Project Book page 17
- Stickers

Lead students to their desks and have them open their Project Book to page 17. Read the labels aloud. Explain to students that they will stick a picture inside each square. Have them look at the stickers on page 69. Encourage students to describe each sticker. Tell them to identify which sticker goes in the *hear* square (the child listening to music). Allow them some time to stick the picture then. Do the same with the other stickers. Walk around and check if students are doing the task appropriately.

DIFFERENTIATED INSTRUCTION

BELOW LEVEL
Look and say.

Materials and preparation
- Project Book page 17

After students have placed the stickers, read out the verbs again and have them repeat.

ABOVE LEVEL

After students have glued the stickers, have them say sentences that describe the pictures. Elicit from them, *She can smell her food.; She can touch the ball.*; etc.

CLOSING

Saying goodbye

Say *goodbye* to each student individually and ask them to say what their favorite part of the class was.

LOOK, LISTEN, AND CIRCLE. WHAT CAN YOU TASTE? WHAT CAN YOU SMELL? 👁️ 👂 ✏️

STEAM • WHAT PARTS OF YOUR BODY HELP YOU FEEL? • UNIT 2   19

Learning goals
- Differentiate the concept of hot and cold food items
- Explore a food tasting experience
- Differentiate taste from smell
- Build a bar graph

STEAM subjects
- Science
- Technology
- Math

Thinking skills
Deciding, separating, exploring, verifying, distinguishing, creating

Main language content
Adjectives: *cold, hot*
I prefer (cold) drinks.
I eat (cold) ice cream.
I like/don't like it.
I can (feel leaves).

OPENING

Circle time

Materials and preparation
- Visual schedule pictures

Say *hello* to students and invite them to sit in a circle. Show them the visual schedule pictures and explain what they are for. Say, *These pictures show our schedule for the day. Let's check them out.* Show all pictures, one at a time, and teach students the name of the subjects. Ask them to say what kind of things they may learn in these subjects and help them understand a little more about them.

> **Note to teachers**
> Call on a student to be the class helper of the day. Tell this student to help you with materials and other simple tasks throughout today's lesson.

Science and technology – Hot or cold?

Materials and preparation
- Computer and projector
- Juice and tea (or any other two snacks, one cold and the other warm)
- Pictures of hot and cold food items

Bring the drinks to class. Have students try the drinks at different temperatures and say the differences. Have them state their preferences. Ask, *Do you prefer hot or cold drinks?* Elicit from students the different food we eat at different temperatures. Ask them, *Do you eat cold pasta? Do you eat hot ice cream?* Invite students to play Kahoot. Access the site https://kahoot.com/ (accessed on August 27, 2019) and follow the instructions. Place images of cold and hot food items in the game and have students click on the word HOT or COLD accordingly. If the use of technology is not possible, invite students to sit at their tables and divide them into pairs. Hand them the images. Have them classify the images into which ones we normally eat hot and which we eat cold. Have them say the words *hot* and *cold* as they classify them.

> **Note to teachers**
> Make sure you have checked with families that no students have food restrictions to the drinks and food items you will use in this lesson.

ACTIVE LEARNING

Science – Guessing and checking

Materials and preparation

- Blindfolds
- Different food items to smell (orange, herbs, cheese, ginger, strawberries, chocolate, coffee powder)

Divide students into groups of three. Blindfold the members of one group. Have another group of three students choose a food item, place it close to the noses of the students who are blindfolded, and invite them to smell it. Have them guess which food it is. Then place the food in their mouths to taste it or have them smell it. Have them confirm their guesses. Review the language chunks and encourage students to use them: *It is (cheese). I like it.; It is (coffee powder) I don't like it.*

Science – Look, listen, and circle. What can you taste? What can you smell?

Materials and preparation

- Colored pencils or crayons
- Project Book page 19

Lead students to their desks. Have them open their Project Book to page 19 and look at the pictures. Encourage them to name the images they see. Help them with the new language. Introduce the words by saying them twice and asking students to repeat. Write them on the board for their reference, too. Then have students identify and circle in blue the things we can taste. Then ask them which of the things portrayed in the images we can smell, but not taste. Have them circle them in green. Walk around and check students' books.

DIFFERENTIATED INSTRUCTION

BELOW LEVEL
Check the book and create sentences.

Materials and preparation

- Project Book page 19

In pairs, students check each other's book. Have them say, *I can smell (perfume); I can taste…*

ABOVE LEVEL

Materials and preparation

- Project Book page 19

In pairs, students check each other's book. Have them say, *I can smell (perfume) with my nose; I can taste (popcorn) with my mouth.* Then ask students to think of two new items for each verb and create sentences, too.

CLOSING

Math – Creating a bar graph

Materials and preparation

- Juice and tea

Review the topic discussed at the beginning of the class. Invite students to build a bar graph. Make a survey among the class. Have them raise their hand if they prefer hot drinks. Have them say, *I prefer hot drinks.* Again, have them raise their hands if they prefer cold drinks. Have them say, *I prefer cold drinks.* Build the graph with them on the board and have them analyze it. You can draw small circles one on top of the other to make a bar in the graph, each circle representing a preference. Ask them, *Do students in this class mostly prefer hot or cold drinks?*

Saying goodbye

Materials and preparation

- Audio library - songs

Have students sing the *Goodbye song* (track 03) with you. Say *goodbye* to them and have them say *goodbye* to you.

Unit 3 Why is your family important to you?

Learning goals
- Explore heritage
- Identify and classify family members
- Identify and color live-in family members
- Share information about live-in family members

STEAM subjects
- Science
- Arts

Thinking skills
Recalling, classifying, ordering, identifying relationships and patterns

Main language content
Family: *aunt, brother, cousin, dad, grandma, grandpa, mom, sister, uncle*

OPENING

Circle time

Materials and preparation
- Visual schedule pictures

Say *hello* to students and invite them to sit in a circle. Show them the visual schedule pictures and explain what they are for. Say, *These pictures show our schedule for the day. Let's check them out!* Show all pictures, one at a time, and teach students the name of the subjects. Ask them to say what kind of things they may learn in these subjects and help them understand a little more about them.

> **Note to teachers**
> You can print out pictures of students doing these activities and use them for the visual schedule.

Science – Genealogy: exploring our heritage

Materials and preparation
- Flashcards: *aunt, brother, cousins, dad, grandma, grandpa, mom, sister, uncle*
- Index cards with family members written on them – one family member on each index card (prepared by you before class starts)
- Masking tape
- Pictures of your own family, including one picture of yourself

Place the pictures of your own family, in no specific order, in the middle of the circle on the floor. Tell students they are all members of your family. Point to your grandpa and ask, *Who is this?* Elicit the answer. Ask, *Do you know his name?* Let students make some guesses and then say your grandfather's name. Place your grandfather's picture on top of the left side of the board, place the *grandpa* index card under the picture, and write your grandfather's name right below the index card. Then ask, *Where is my grandma?* Let students hand the picture of your grandmother to you, ask for her name, and then place this picture beside your grandfather's. Place the *grandma* index card under the picture and write your grandmother's name below the index card. Repeat this procedure until they have identified all the members in your family.

Place each picture as if you were building your family tree, but do not mention this to the students. Keep the pictures in position on the board.

> **Note to teachers**
>
> It's possible that not all students come from a traditional family setting.
>
> Before starting, ask students
> - *What makes a family?*
> - *How are families the same and different?*
>
> Make it clear that families come in many different forms. Make sure there is no mocking of those coming from non-traditional family sets. Also, do not express any kind of judgment and discourage any controversial conversation.

ACTIVE LEARNING

Arts – Classifying family members

Materials and preparation

- Colored pencils

On the right side of the board, draw a simple house and write *My house* on top of it. Say, *I live here* and write it on the board. Take your own picture from the left side of the board and place it next to or inside the house. Take the picture of one of your parents or relatives, show it to the students, and say, *My sister* (for example) *lives here. We live together.* Write the sentences on the board. Then place your sister's picture and the *sister* index card near your picture in the house. Repeat the procedure until you have placed all those who live with you in the house. Draw another house and ask a volunteer to do the same, using your family pictures as if they were his or hers.

Science and arts – Identify the family members.

Materials and preparation

- Colored pencils
- Project Book page 21

Lead students to their desks. Have them open their Project Book to page 21 and look at the pictures. Encourage them to say the family members on the leaves. Explain that they are going to color only the family members who live together with them, in the same house. Tell them to use the empty leaf to draw somebody who lives with them, but is not already drawn on the leaves. You may also help them write the word for that family member.

DIFFERENTIATED INSTRUCTION

BELOW LEVEL
Science and arts – Sharing information about my live-in family members

Materials and preparation

- Project Book page 21

In pairs, students share their live-in family members. They point to the pictures they have colored and name them. Walk around, monitor the activity, and help them as needed.

ABOVE LEVEL

In pairs, students share their live-in family members and take turns saying sentences like, *My mother and I live together. My baby sister, my brother, and I live together.* Walk around, monitor the activity, and help them as needed.

CLOSING

Saying goodbye

Say *goodbye* to students and have them say *goodbye* to you and to their classmates.

> **Note to teachers**
>
> Ask students to bring a doll, an action figure, a puppet, or a stuffed animal for next class.

Unit 3

Learning goals
- Explore heritage
- Identify family members
- Draw family members and place them accordingly in a family tree
- Build a family tree

STEAM subjects
- Science
- Arts
- Math

Thinking skills
Recalling, classifying, ordering, identifying relationships and patterns

Main language content
Family: *aunt, brother, cousin, dad, grandma, grandpa, mom, sister, uncle*
How many (brothers)?
There are (two brothers).

OPENING

Circle time

Materials and preparation
- Visual schedule pictures

Say *hello* to students and invite them to sit in a circle. Show them the visual schedule pictures and explain what they are for. Say, *These pictures show our schedule for the day. Let's check them out!* Show all pictures, one at a time, and teach students the name of the subjects. Ask them to say what kind of things they may learn in these subjects and help them understand a little more about them.

> **Note to teachers**
> You can print out pictures of students doing these activities and use them for the visual schedule.

Science – Anthropology: identifying relationships and patterns in human behavior

Materials and preparation
- Students' toys

Have students sit in a circle, each one holding the toy they brought from home. Say that they are going to travel to *Imagination Land* and ask, *What if you were your mom/dad?* Explain to students that they are going to demonstrate, with their toys, what they would do and how they would act if they were their mom or dad. Also, explain that *What if* questions are not about facts, real things, but about possibilities, imagination, and creativity. Encourage students to be creative and nice. Invite some volunteers to collaborate and then ask other questions, like *What if you were (a classmate's) sister/brother?* Proceed like this, changing questions, until all students have participated at least once.

ACTIVE LEARNING

Science and arts – Build your family tree.

Materials and preparation
- Craft paper – white: one for each student
- Crepe paper – brown: enough for students to cover the trunk and branches of the tree
- Glue
- Project Book page 23
- Project Book page 21 from previous class
- Scissors

Have students open their Project Book to page 23 and tell them to guess what they are going to do. Instruct them to cut out the tree and cover the trunk and branches with the brown crepe paper. They can choose how to do it: one single plain layer, many small crumpled pieces, one crumpled piece for each branch and so on. While waiting for the glue to dry, have students open their Project Book to page 21 and cut out the leaves they colored in the previous class. Help them glue the tree to the chart paper. Then help them glue the leaves onto the tree, placing each drawing in the correct place.

Math – sorting, ordering, and classifying

Materials and preparation
- Blank Bingo cards – one for each student (prepared before class)
- Crayons

Prior to the lesson, prepare a blank bingo chart for each student. It should be a piece of paper divided into six squares – two columns with three squares each. Explain to the students that you are going to play *Bingo*. Make sure all students are familiar with the concept of the game. Hand them the cards. On the board, write down the words *mom, dad, sister, brother, grandma, grandpa, aunt, uncle, son, daughter*. Say the words aloud as you write them and have students repeat them before you move on to the next word. Ask students which of these family members are children and which ones are adults. Underline them with different colors of chalk or marker. Tell students to silently choose the names of three children out of the family members you wrote on the board and help students write them down in the first column, one in each square. Repeat the procedure for three adults in the second column. Once all students have their cards correctly prepared, tell them you are going to say a word at random, and, if they have this word on their card, they have to circle it with a crayon. When they have circled all the names on their card, they should say *Bingo!* Say the first word and allow some time for students to circle it before moving on to the next. Continue until someone says *Bingo*. The students who say it first should help their classmates find the words on their cards so that they can say them, too. Go on until you have said all of the words and all the students have a chance to say *Bingo!*

DIFFERENTIATED INSTRUCTION

BELOW LEVEL
Science and math – Exploring our heritage and counting

Materials and preparation
- Your own (or somebody else's) family tree

Show students your own family tree, count the number of male members, and say, *There are… men in my house*. Do the same with the female members. Write the two sentences on the board for students' reference. Ask students to count the people in their family the same way you did and share the information in pairs.

ABOVE LEVEL

Show students your own family tree, count the number of male members, and say, *There are… men in my house*. Do the same with the female members. Write the two sentences on the board for students' reference. Ask students to count the people in their family the same way you did and share the information in pairs. After that, tell them to ask each other, *How many people are there in your house?* Elicit, *There are (five) people in my house*.

CLOSING

Saying goodbye

Say *goodbye* to each student individually and ask them to say what their favorite part of the class was. Say, *See you tomorrow* and have them say it back to you.

CIRCLE WHAT YOU CAN DO BY YOURSELF. CATEGORIZE, CUT, AND GLUE.

COOK

MAKE THE BED

PLAY

WASH THE DISHES

FEED THE PETS

BUY THINGS

STEAM • WHY IS YOUR FAMILY IMPORTANT TO YOU? • UNIT 3   25

Learning goals
- Recognize and categorize actions
- Learn and draw one
- Compare and contrast actions

STEAM subjects
- Arts
- Math

Thinking skills
Observing, recalling, organizing, analyzing, categorizing

Main language content
Actions: *cook, make the bed, play, wash the dishes, feed the pets, buy things*

OPENING

Circle time

Materials and preparation
- Visual schedule pictures

Say *hello* to students and invite them to sit in a circle. Show them the visual schedule pictures and explain what they are for. Say, *These pictures show our schedule for the day. Let's check them out!* Show all pictures, one at a time, and teach students the name of the subjects. Ask them to say what kind of things they may learn in these subjects and help them understand a little more about them.

> **Note to teachers**
> You can print out pictures of students doing these activities and use them for the visual schedule.

Math – Recognizing and categorizing actions

Materials and preparation
- Student's Book

Tell students you are going to talk about actions today. Have them skim their Student's Book for an action and say it aloud. In the middle of the board, write the actions they mention, say them aloud, and invite them all to repeat. Go on until they cannot recognize any more actions in the book. Help them find some others, if necessary. On the top of the left side of the board, write *fun*. Write *chore* on the top of the right side. Then read the first action on the board and ask, *Do you do it for fun or is it a chore?* Invite students to come to the board and draw a tally mark on the correct side of the table according to how they categorized the action.
After that, have students count how many there are in each of the columns.

28 STEAM

ACTIVE LEARNING

Arts and math – Drawing a Venn diagram

Materials and preparation
- Crayons or colored pencils
- White poster paper (one sheet per pair of students)

Lead students to their desks. Explain that there are many different ways to categorize, compare, or contrast things. One of them is by making a list, just like you did on the board during the previous activity using two different categories – fun and chore actions. We can also use charts or diagrams. Tell them that they are going to draw a diagram where they can insert three different categories. You do not need to tell them the name of the diagram. Erase the middle of the board and draw an example of the Venn diagram using two circles and one intersection. Use different colors for each circle. Highlight the intersection using a brighter color. Draw another Venn diagram using two other shapes. Tell them not to think about the items they are going to place in the diagram for now. Divide them into pairs and and hand students a sheet of poster paper and some crayons or colored pencils. Tell them to draw their diagrams using any shape, as long as they come out with three spaces about the same size: two separate spaces and one intersection. When they are finished, collect their work and name the spaces for the next activity: space 1: *kids*; space 2: *adults*; intersection: *adults and kids*. You may have students write only the initial letters K, A, and AK.

> **Note to teachers**
> Venn diagrams can be used effectively by younger students. The trick is to make them user-friendly, hands-on, and developmentally appropriate as a tool even kindergarten students can use with ease. There are many uses for the Venn diagram and you can search the Internet for ideas on how to make the best of it for students.

Arts and math – Circle and categorize the family activities.

Materials and preparation
- Colored pencils
- Glue
- Project Book page 25
- Scissors
- Venn diagram produced during the previous activity

Have students open their Project Book to page 25 and look at the pictures. Invite volunteers to read the labels and help them with vocabulary and pronunciation. Instruct them to circle the activities they do by themselves, the ones performed by their parents, and the ones they do together with their parents. They are not supposed to circle the activities not performed by themselves and/or their tutors. Allow students some time to circle the pictures. Then, tell them to cut out all the pictures and glue them to the corresponding space in the diagram.

DIFFERENTIATED INSTRUCTION

BELOW LEVEL
Math – Counting, comparing, and contrasting

Materials and preparation
- Students' activities diagram

Have students count how many activities they placed in each space. In pairs, students compare the number of activities in each space and say who performs the greater number of activities.

ABOVE LEVEL

Have students count how many activities they placed in each space. In pairs, students compare the number of activities in each space and say who performs the greater number of activities, whose parents perform more activities, and who performs more activities together with their parents.

CLOSING

Saying goodbye

Say *goodbye* to each student individually and ask them to say what their favorite part of the class was. Say, *See you tomorrow* and have them say it back to you.

**ORDER THE ACTIVITIES.
MAKE AN ACTIVITY CLOCK.**

Learning goals
- Recall daily activities and put them in chronological order
- Build a paper clock

STEAM subjects
- Engineering
- Arts
- Math

Thinking skills
Observing, recalling, comparing, ordering, analyzing, categorizing

Main language content
Daily activities: *brush your teeth, cook, go to school, make the bed, play, sleep*

OPENING

Circle time

Materials and preparation
- Visual schedule pictures

Say *hello* to students and invite them to sit in a circle. Show them the visual schedule pictures and explain what they are for. Say, *These pictures show our schedule for the day. Let's check them out!* Show all pictures, one at a time, and teach students the name of the subjects. Ask them to say what kind of things they may learn in these subjects and help them understand a little more about them.

> **Note to teachers**
> Call on a student to be the class helper of the day. Tell this student to help you with materials and other simple tasks throughout today's lesson.

Arts and math – Recognizing, categorizing, and miming

Review with students the Venn diagram from the previous class, focusing on the actions they perform by themselves. Write them on the board. Invite students to think of actions they perform by themselves every day. Write them down on the board, too. You may refer to the *fun* and *chore* lists from the previous class for more examples. Choose one of the activities and ask, *When do you (activity)? In the morning?* Once you have a few examples of everyday activities, invite students to mime some of them.

ACTIVE LEARNING

Arts – Gesturing and dancing along to a song

Materials and preparation
- *Mulberry Bush* nursery rhyme video/audio (from an online source)

Tell students that they are going to listen to a song about activities we do in the morning. Play the *Mulberry Bush* nursery rhyme once without pauses so students can get a feel for the rhythm. As the activities are mentioned in the lyrics, use hand gestures to mimic them. Play the song again, mime the actions, and encourage students to do the same thing. Repeat one more time so students are comfortable with the song and can sing and/or dance along to the melody. (Alternatively, play the song once or twice for students to learn the rhythm, then read the lyrics to them, changing some sentences to make it easier – for example, you may leave out *Here we go round the mulberry bush,* and also substitute *This is the way we drink our milk* for *This is the way we comb our hair.*)

Note to teachers
Mulberry Bush nursery rhyme lyrics:

Here we go round the mulberry bush, the mulberry bush, the mulberry bush
Here we go round the mulberry bush, so early in the morning
This is the way we brush our teeth, we brush our teeth, we brush our teeth
This is the way we brush our teeth, so early in the morning
This is the way we wash our face, we wash our face, we wash our face
This is the way we wash our face, so early in the morning
This is the way we comb our hair, we comb our hair, we comb our hair
This is the way we comb our hair, so early in the morning
This is the way we dress for school, we dress for school, we dress for school
This is the way we dress for school, so early in the morning
This is the way we go to school, we go to school, we go to school
This is the way we go to school, so early in the morning

Engineering and math – Order the activities and build an activity clock.

Materials and preparation
- Adhesive tape
- Cardboard circles the size of the clock students are going to build – one for each student (prepared before class)
- Glue
- Hole punch
- Paper clock hands – one for each student (prepared before class)
- Paper fasteners – one for each student
- Project Book page 27
- Scissors
- String

Before class, cut a circle of cardboard for each student, with a radius slightly larger than the side of the slices in Project Book page 27. Poke a hole in the middle of each circle. Also, cut an arrow out of cardboard (one for each student) and the string into pieces roughly the same size as the radius of the circle.

Lead students to their desks. Tell them that they are going to build an activity clock. Have them cut out the illustrations in Project Book page 27 and point out how they look like parts of a circle. Ask students to identify the activity in each slide (*make the bed, go to school, play, help in the kitchen, brush the teeth, go to bed*). Write them on the board and have students copy them into the correct slices. Then tell them to number the activities from 1-6 in the order that they perform them daily. After they are done, hand out the cardboard circles and tell students to position each slice in order, filling the circle. Walk around the classroom to check that they are doing it correctly and help them glue the pieces in place.

Hand out the arrows, the paper fasteners, and the string. Tell students that the arrow is meant to be the hand of the clock. Use a hole punch to make a hole and help them attach it to the hole in the center with the paper fastener. Tell students that they can hang this activity clock from their bedroom walls. In order to do that, help them attach the string to the back of their clock using tape. Encourage students to use the clock at home, moving the arrow to indicate what activity they are supposed to do at each given time.

(Alternatively, bring the clock all set to class so students have more time to position the activities and share with the whole class the order they do each one.)

DIFFERENTIATED INSTRUCTION

BELOW LEVEL
Arts – Using images to represent lyrics from a song; putting new words to an established rhythm

Materials and preparation
- Students' activity clock

Ask students, *Which activities from the song are also on your clock?* Explain that you are about to sing the song again. This time, students should use the hand of their clock to point to the activities when they are mentioned in the song.

ABOVE LEVEL

Ask students, *Which activities from the song are also on your clock?* Explain that you are about to sing the song again, but with the activities on the clock. Practice a few times with the new lyrics and then sing your new version of the song together as a group.

CLOSING

Saying goodbye

Materials and preparation
- Audio library - songs

Have students sing the *Goodbye song* (track 03) with you. Say *goodbye* to them and have them say *goodbye* to you and their classmates.

Unit 4 What happens to your body when you are hot or cold?

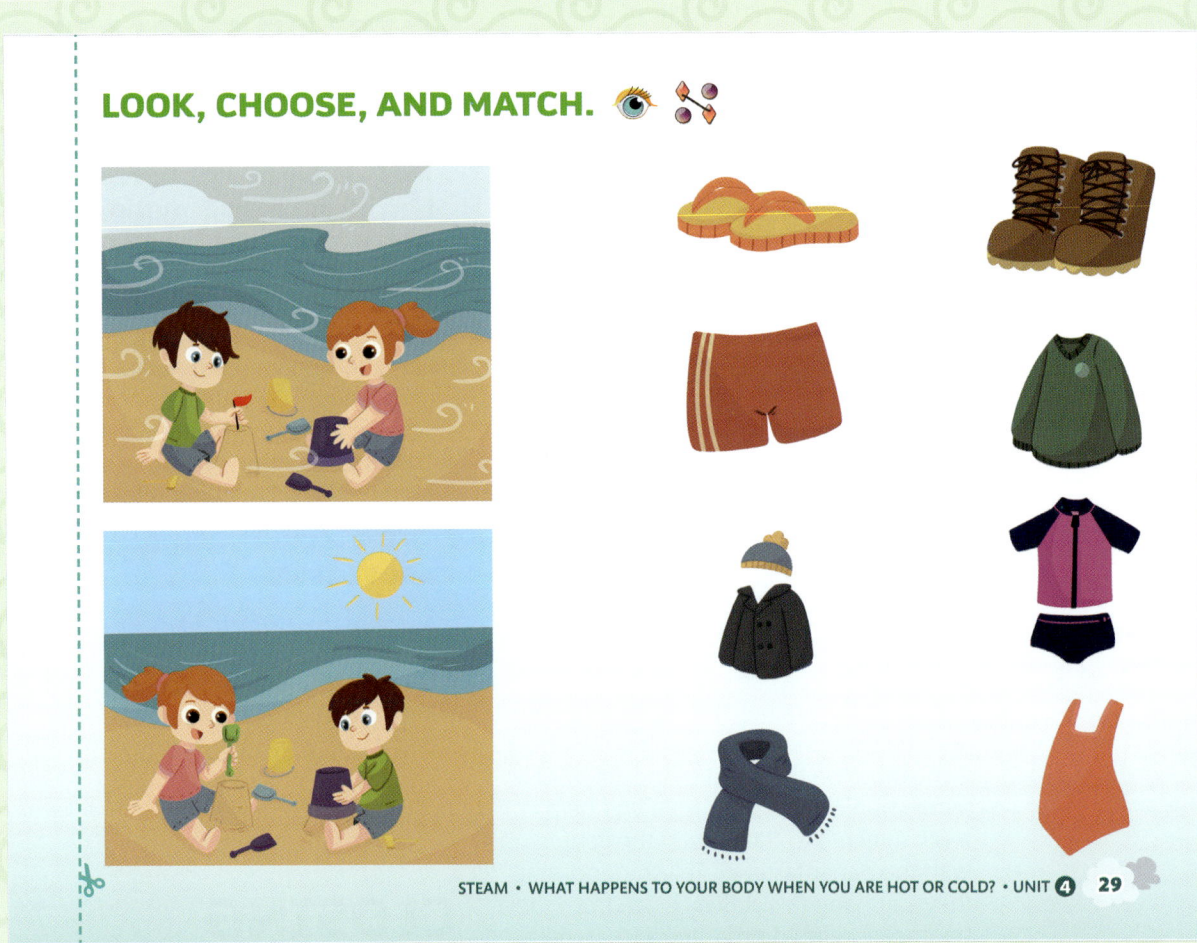

OPENING

Circle time

Materials and preparation
- Visual schedule pictures

Say *hello* to students and invite them to sit in a circle. Show them the visual schedule pictures and explain what they are for. Say, *These pictures show our schedule for the day. Let's check them out!* Show all pictures, one at a time, and teach students the name of the subjects. Ask them to say what kind of things they may learn in these subjects and help them understand a little more about them.

> **Note to teachers**
> You can print out pictures of students doing these activities and use them for the visual schedule.

Technology - Searching for different kinds of beaches

Materials and preparation
- Computer with access to the internet
- Projector or television

Ask students to talk about any experiences they have had at the beach. If they have never been to the beach, ask them if they have seen pictures or would like to visit one. Invite students to say what they can find at the beach.
Take students somewhere in the school where there is a computer and a projector or television. Explain that they will learn how to look up things online today. As if anyone has had any experience searching things online or if they know of any search engines they can use. Choose a search engine they mention/of your choice and say, *I want to find different beaches around the world. How can I do that? Can you help me?* Brainstorm ideas and allow a few students to help you type the word *beaches* with your help. Go on by asking them about the next steps to find these images (click *enter*, scroll down the page, etc.). Help as needed. Click on the pictures to zoom in on them and allow students to comment on the pictures. You may also search for the word *cold* and have them help you with the steps.

Learning goals
- Learn to use a search engine
- Search the internet for pictures of beaches
- Sort out clothing items
- Draw and talking about their favorite kind of beach
- Retell a story

STEAM subjects
- Technology
- Arts
- Math

Thinking skills
Remembering, identifying, sorting, comparing, contrasting, understanding, applying, analyzing, creating, retelling

Main language content
Computer language: *click, computer, look up, scroll down*
Clothes: *bikini, boots, coat, flip-flops, scarf, shorts, sweater, swimming suit*
I like beaches with (white sand).
It's hot/cold. I'll put on my (coat).

Note to teachers
When teaching students the steps to work with a technological device, make sure to allow them to do part of the procedures themselves and then try doing it all by themselves once. Practice is the best way to learn.

ACTIVE LEARNING

Arts and math – Look, choose, and match.

Materials and preparation
- Colored pencils (orange and blue)
- Project Book page 29

Students open their Project Book to page 29. Elicit from them the clothing items illustrated on the top of the page. Write the words on the board as students mention them. Draw their attention to the two big pictures and encourage them to say what's different between them. You can ask them questions, if you prefer. Suggested questions are, *What's the weather like in this picture? Is the water calm or rough?* Tell students they will sort the clothing items according to the weather portrayed in each picture. Ask them to draw an orange line from the hot weather clothes to the children on the sunny day and a blue line from the cold weather clothes to the children on the cold day. For correction, students say, *It's hot. I'll put on my flip-flops.; It's cold. I'll put on my boots.*, etc. Model first. Write the sentences on the board for students' reference.

Arts – My favorite kind of beach

Materials and preparation
- Colored pencils or crayons
- Sheets of paper

Ask students, *Have you ever been to the beach? Do you like going to the beach? What kind of beach do you prefer? What do you like doing on the beach?* Help them with vocabulary. Distribute the materials and tell them they are going to draw themselves on their favorite kind of beach. Remind students to draw the appropriate pieces of clothing according to the weather they choose. Walk around and praise their work.

Note to teachers
If there are students who have never been to the beach, encourage them to create the beach they would like to be on.

DIFFERENTIATED INSTRUCTION

BELOW LEVEL
Share and talk about drawings.

Materials and preparation
- Students' drawings

In pairs, students share and talk about their drawings.

ABOVE LEVEL

In pairs, students share and talk about their drawings. Then students take turns sharing and describing their classmate's drawing to the whole class.

CLOSING

Retelling a story

Materials and preparation
- Big Book Unit 4: *A vacation on the beach*

Show students the Big Book story and have them help you retell the story as a class. Help them by pointing at the illustrations.

Saying goodbye

Materials and preparation
- Puppet

Using the puppet, ask students what they liked most in today's class. Say *goodbye* to them and have them say *goodbye* to you and to the puppet.

Learning goals
- Group animals according to where they live
- Learn that some sea animals live on the land, too
- Learn about power buttons in technological devices and their colors

STEAM subjects
- Science
- Technology
- Arts
- Math

Thinking skills
Remembering, sorting

Main language content
Crab, dolphins, fish, octopus, shark, shell, starfish, turtle
Where do sharks live? They live in the ocean.

OPENING

Circle time

Materials and preparation
- Visual schedule pictures

Say *hello* to students and invite them to sit in a circle. Show them the visual schedule pictures and explain what they are for. Say, *These pictures show our schedule for the day. Let's check them out!* Show all pictures, one at a time, and teach students the name of the subjects. Ask them to say what kind of things they may learn in these subjects and help them understand a little more about them.

> **Note to teachers**
> You can print out pictures of students doing these activities and use them for the visual schedule.

Science and math - Sea animals that go to the land

Materials and preparation
- Pictures of the following animals: crab, dolphin, fish, octopus, shark, turtle

Place the cards in the middle of the circle. Invite one student at a time to stand up and grab one card and show to their classmates, who will name the animal. Ask, *Do (turtles) live in the sea or in the sea and on the land?* Ask students if they have ever seen a frog out of water. Then say that turtles live part of their lives in the sea and part of it on land. Repeat with the other cards.
Have students group the cards according to where the animals live, in the sea or both in the sea and on the land. Ask them to count how many of each there are.

ACTIVE LEARNING

Science and arts – Color the animals that live both on the land and in the sea.

Materials and preparation
- Project Book page 31

Lead students to their desks and have students open their Project Book to page 31. Show them each of the pictures and have them name the animals. Tell students they will only color the sea animals that live both on land and in the sea. Allow them to discuss their opinions and knowledge about sea animals with a classmate before starting coloring. When correcting the activity, ask, *How many animals are there? How many of these animals never leave the sea?* Elicit that only the crab and the turtle can move to land.

> **Note to teachers**
>
> If you have laptops, tablets, or computers available, you can invite students to play the game *Animals in the ocean*, available at http://www.sheppardsoftware.com/preschool/animals/ocean/animaloceanfindcountgame.htm (accessed on September 1, 2019) in small groups. Show them how to play first. Review the language while you play: names of the animals, numbers, and colors.

Technology – Play *Crabs on, crabs off*.

Materials and preparation
- Masking tape
- Two pictures of a power button, one colored red and another one colored blue

Use tape to place both pictures on the wall. Ask students if they can recognize that picture. If they say *yes*, ask them where they have seen it. They might mention a computer, tablet, phone, or another electronic gadget. You may also show them this button in a device available in the school.

After students have understood that this button turns something on and off, ask them if they know what the colors represent. If nobody can answer this, invite a student to pretend to click on the "buttons" and say that you are a robot controlled by those buttons. As they click the blue button, start moving like a robot; when they click the red button, pretend to be "off", close your eyes and stop moving. Then play the game with the students. Have them stand up and say, *You are all robot crabs.* When *someone clicks the "on" button, you will move with your legs wide open; when the off button is clicked, you must stop moving and stand still.* Have different students be the ones controlling the crab robots.

DIFFERENTIATED INSTRUCTION

BELOW LEVEL
Draw an animal. Say where it lives.

Materials and preparation
- Pencils
- Sheets of paper (one per student)

Ask students to draw an animal of their choice. Then have them work in pairs and take turns showing their animals to their classmate, who will say its name and where they can see it: in the sea, on land, or in the sky.

ABOVE LEVEL

Do the procedures explained in *Below level*, but after students finish talking about their classmate's drawing, have them divide the drawings into three categories according to where they can see those animals. Invite them to count how many animals there are in each category.

CLOSING

Saying goodbye

Say *goodbye* to students and have them say *goodbye* to you and their classmates.

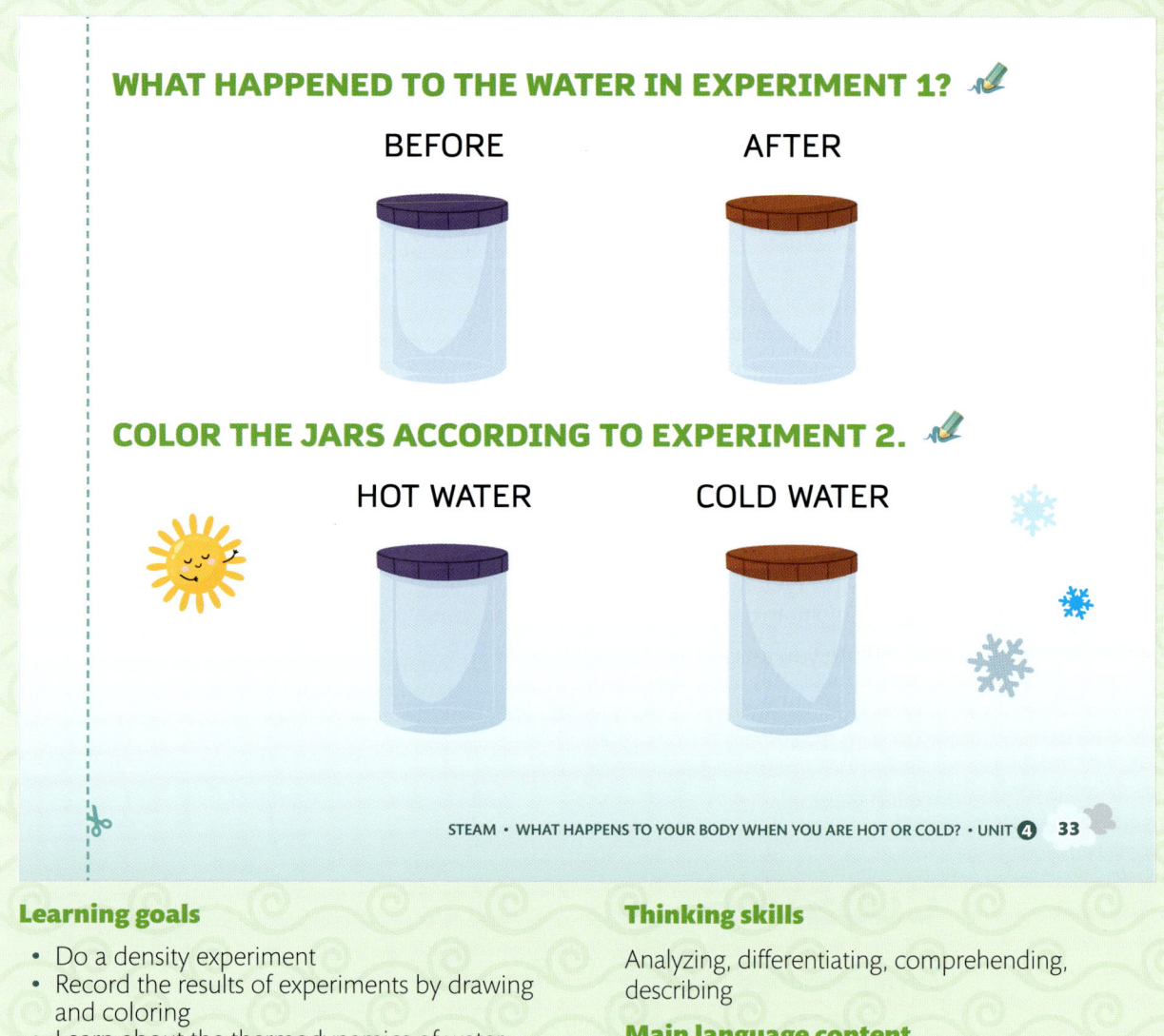

Learning goals
- Do a density experiment
- Record the results of experiments by drawing and coloring
- Learn about the thermodynamics of water

STEAM subjects
- Science
- Technology

Thinking skills
Analyzing, differentiating, comprehending, describing

Main language content
Words for the experiment: *cold, container, hot, water*
What is your hypothesis?
It will increase. It will decrease.

OPENING

Circle time

Materials and preparation
- Visual schedule pictures

Say *hello* to students and invite them to sit in a circle. place the visual schedule pictures face down in the circle. Say one of the subjects students will have in today's class and have them take turns turning over the cards and looking for the one representing that day's schedule. When both pictures have been found, have a volunteer place them somewhere in the room where everyone can see the schedule.

> **Note to teachers**
> You can also use a rhyme to talk about the schedule.
> **T:** *Today our class has two parts, one has science and the other has...*
> **S:** *Arts!*

Science – Hot or cold?

Materials and preparation
- Pictures of sunny, cold, snowy, and rainy places

Show students the images one at a time. Have them identify whether they depict hot or cold places. Encourage them to say *hot* or *cold* accordingly. Ask students if they prefer hot or cold weather. Then ask them what kind of temperature they like to take their showers at.

36 STEAM

ACTIVE LEARNING

Science – Hot and cold water: density experiment

Materials and preparation
- Three containers
- An elastic band (or a marker)
- Cold and hot water
- Food coloring

Invite students to do two experiments with hot and cold water. Explain that you will ask this question throughout the experiments: *What is your hypothesis?* Ask them if they have ever heard this word and say, *This word is used when we want to imagine the result for something.* Use a hypothesis to exemplify: *Let's imagine we all have no teeth. What can we eat? Can we eat meat?* Allow students to think of possibilities to this imaginary situation and share with the class. Then say, *See? These imaginary ideas are all hypotheses.* Students will carry out experiment 1 and while they wait for the result, they will carry out experiment 2.

> **Note to teachers**
> Take students to the science lab, school kitchen, or a room near the kitchen. You will need the freezer.

EXPERIMENT 1
Have students fill a container with cold water. Have them place an elastic band to mark the level of the water (you can also use a marker). Tell students they will place the container with water in the freezer, until the water is completely frozen. Ask them, *Will the level of the water increase or decrease? What is your hypothesis?* Moving the palm of your hand up or down, teach them the main language and encourage them to say, *It will increase. It will decrease.* Carry out experiment 2 with them while the water is in the freezer. Later, take the container out of the freezer and have students observe what happened. Ask if their hypothesis was correct and have them use their own words to report the results to class.

EXPERIMENT 2
Fill two containers with water — one with hot water and one with cold water. Tell students you will add food coloring to both containers. Ask them, *What do you think will happen? What is your hypothesis?* Give them some time to discuss and think about it. Invite a student to drop blue food coloring into the cold water and invite another student to drop red food coloring into the other container. Tell all the students to observe carefully and tell you what they see. The food coloring in the cold water will move more slowly and the red coloring will move faster because the water molecules in hot water have more energy, so they move faster.

DIFFERENTIATED INSTRUCTION

BELOW LEVEL
Science and arts – What happened to the water in experiment 1? Color the jars according to experiment 2.

Materials and preparation
- Colored pencils
- Pencils
- Project Book page 33

Lead students to their desks and have them open their Project Book to page 31. Explain that the page is divided into two parts — on the top of the page they will record what happened in experiment 1; at the bottom they will record what happened in experiment 2. Before you assign the task, review with students what each experiment was about and the procedures taken in each of them.

ABOVE LEVEL
Tell students to do the procedures explained in *Below level*. After that, in pairs, have students take turns explaining each experiment. Student A explains experiment 1; Student B explains experiment 2. Walk around, monitor, and help them as needed.

CLOSING

Check the experiments.
Have students sit in a circle. Ask them to talk about both experiments and the results of their experiments. Have them also give their opinion on today's class activities.

Saying goodbye
Materials and preparation
- Audio library – songs

Have students stand up and invite everybody to sing the *Goodbye song* (track 03) while waving at each goodbye at each other.

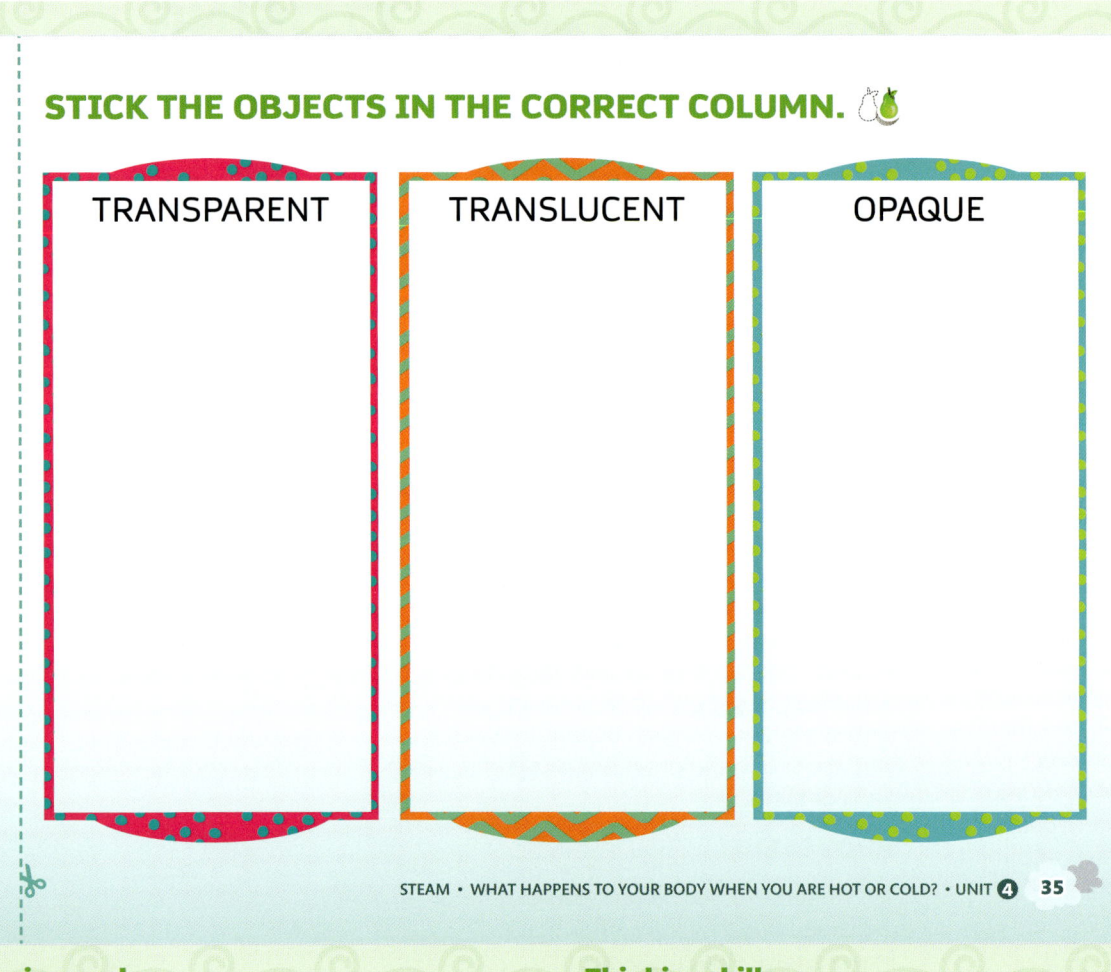

Learning goals
- Talk about sunny and cloudy days
- Understand the concept of shadows
- Classify objects into cold and hot

STEAM subjects
- Science
- Math

Thinking skills
Understanding, applying, analyzing, classifying

Main language content
Flashlight, opaque, shadow, shapes, sun, transparent, translucent
What is your hypothesis?
It's a bunny. It's a crocodile.
Books are opaque. Plastic bottles are transparent.

OPENING

Circle time

Materials and preparation
- Visual schedule pictures

Say *hello* to students and invite them to sit in a circle. Show them the visual schedule pictures and explain what they are for. Say, *These pictures show our schedule for the day. Let's check them out!* Show all pictures, one at a time, and teach students the name of the subjects. Ask them to say what kind of things they may learn in these subjects and help them understand a little more about them.

> **Note to teachers**
> You can use a bell and the rhyme to introduce the schedule:
> **T:** *Can you hear the chime?*
> **S:** *It's (science) time!*

Science – Making shadows

Materials and preparation
- Flashlight
- Objects from the classroom

Have students remain in the circle. Darken the room. Using the flashlight, shine the light on the wall. Use your hands to make different shapes on the wall. Learn how to make animals (hold up two fingers to make a bunny, make a gesture as if you are cutting something with scissors to make a crocodile, etc.). Have students guess the different shapes. Encourage them to say, *It's a bunny. It's a crocodile.* Use other objects and have students guess. Encourage them to say what they see. Ask students what they think might happen to the shadows when you move the objects closer to the flashlight or further from the flashlight. Ask them, *What is your hypothesis? How does the distance from the light change the shape of the shadow?* Have them test and give you the answer. Help them with the vocabulary needed.

ACTIVE LEARNING

Science – Transparent, opaque, or translucent?

Materials and preparation
- Classroom objects (transparent, opaque, and translucent)
- Flashlights (one per pair of students)

Teach students the difference between the words *transparent*, *translucent*, and *opaque*. Elicit from them which objects they think can be classified as *transparent*, *translucent*, and *opaque*. Help them by giving examples. Darken the room again, divide students into pairs, and hand a flashlight to each pair of students. Invite them to go around the classroom and test their hypotheses. Explain to students that light will shine through transparent objects. A little light will pass through translucent objects and no light will pass through opaque objects like books and mugs. Ask them to test and mention at least one object of each kind.

Stick the objects in the correct column.

Materials and preparation
- Project page 35
- Stickers

Lead students to their desks and have them open their Project Book to page 35. Read out the three words and explain what they will have to do. Allow them some time to glue the stickers in the correct column.

DIFFERENTIATED INSTRUCTION

BELOW LEVEL
Science and math – Flashlight shapes

Materials and preparation
- Sheets of craft paper cut into squares, triangles, and circles (one of each, smaller than the lens of the flashlight)
- Flashlights
- Scissors
- Tape

Make shadow shapes by cutting shapes from the cardboard paper. Have students choose from the shapes and name them. Then tape the shapes, one at a time, over the flashlight. Invite students to turn on the flashlight and shine the flashlight at the wall. They will have a shape shadow. Have them say the name of the shape/object.

ABOVE LEVEL

Materials and preparation
- Clothing items and accessories out of cardboard paper (cut them out before class)
- Flashlights
- Scissors
- Tape

After the procedures described above, give students hot and cold weather clothing items and accessories out of cardboard paper and ask students to repeat the procedure. As they shine the flashlight on the wall, review vocabulary and structures. Ask them, for example, *When do you wear flip-flops? In hot weather or in cold weather?*

CLOSING

Saying goodbye

Say *goodbye* to students and have them wave *goodbye*.

Unit 5 Why is it important to take care of our planet?

Learning goals
- Learn about gravity
- Use gravity to create art
- Observe how gravity influences the speed and weight of objects when dropped
- Use mathematics to count paint splats
- Compare shapes and sizes of the paint splats

STEAM subjects
- Science
- Arts
- Math

Thinking skills
Understanding, applying, comparing, analyzing, creating

Main language content
Gravity activities: *astronaut, close, bigger, far, floating, gravity, paint, smaller, space shuttle*
Numbers: 1-21
They're floating. Are they all the same size? There are (three) big splats, (two) medium-sized splats, and (seven) small splats.

OPENING

Circle time

Materials and preparation
- Visual schedule pictures

Say *hello* to students and invite them to sit in a circle. Show them the visual schedule pictures and explain what they are for. Say, *These pictures show our schedule for the day. Let's check them out!* Show all pictures, one at a time, and teach students the name of the subjects. Ask them to say what kind of things they may learn in these subjects and help them understand a little more about them.

Gravity – How come we don't float?

Materials and preparation
- A large piece of magnet
- Metal objects
- Pictures of astronauts floating inside space shuttles

Show students the pictures (have them pass them around) and ask them, *What is the occupation of the people in the pictures? Have you ever seen an astronaut? Where are the people in the pictures? What is happening to them?* Help them with the new language (*astronaut, space shuttle, floating*). Explain that they are floating and ask students why they think they are floating. Explain they are floating because there is no gravity in space. Show them the magnet and ask them what happens when we place a paper clip next to it (the clip sticks to the magnet). Tell them that our planet does the same to us and that is why we do not float around. Explain that this is called *gravity*.

> **Note to teachers**
> You can also show students videos of astronauts in space, especially the ones where they spill water – students will see the water drops floating in the air.

ACTIVE LEARNING

Science - Gravity art

Materials and preparation

- A stool
- Big pompoms
- Brown butcher paper
- Paint
- Sticky tape (indoor activity)
- Weights to hold the butcher paper down (outdoor activity)

Take students outside or make space in the classroom. Tell students that today's project has sound, many colors, and a lot of paint. Ask, *What do you think it will be?* If you are working outdoors, place the butcher paper on the floor and hold it down with weights on the four corners. If you are working in the classroom, use sticky tape to fix it to the classroom floor and make sure that your desk is far from anything that should not get dirty. Show students the pompoms and the paint. Explain that you are going to use the pompoms to create art by dipping them into the paint and then dropping or throwing them onto the butcher paper. Ask, *What do you think will happen on the butcher paper?* Model one example and, slowly, ask one student at a time to try it. After their first attempt, tell them to look at the paper and describe what they see. Have students dip their pompoms into the paint and tell them to stand in different places around the paper to throw them. They can stand on a stool, on the ground, closer to the paper or further away from it. Ask them to identify if anything changes depending on the distance they take.

When students have had their fun from various heights and distances, encourage them to take a closer look at the pompom imprints on the butcher paper. Ask, *Are they all the same size? Did their pompoms make noise when they hit the paper?* (They splatted.) *What shapes can you see? Which splats are bigger and why?* (Pompoms dipped in paint become heavier, so when they are thrown from a higher place they should make bigger splats on the paper because of gravity). Help them with the new language (*big, small, close, far*). Now that students have understood what went on with the height and distance, have them experiment some more if there is time left.

> **Note to teachers**
> For an activity such as this, it is wise to ask students to bring in a big old T-shirt that they can wear over their clothes.

Arts and math – Count the splats on the paintings. Color.

Materials and preparation

- Colored pencils
- Markers
- Project Book page 37

Have students open their Project Book to page 37. Ask them what they see in each painting and which of the paintings on the page looks more like the one they have just made. Ask, *Are they all the same size? How many sizes can you see?* Tell them to count the splats on each painting and color them.

DIFFERENTIATED INSTRUCTION

BELOW LEVEL
Count the splats.

Tell students to sort out the different sizes of splats on the painting they made and count how many of each size there are.

ABOVE LEVEL

Tell students to sort out the different sizes of splats on the painting they made, count how many of each size there are, and write the total number. Elicit from them, *There are (five) big splats, (four) medium-sized splats, and small splats.*

CLOSING

Reflecting

Ask students what they think life would be like if there were no gravity. How would we live? Encourage students to use the prompt *I think (we would float)* to talk about their ideas.

Saying goodbye

Say *goodbye* to students and have them say *goodbye* to you and to their classmates.

STEAM • WHY IS IT IMPORTANT TO TAKE CARE OF OUR PLANET? • UNIT 5   39

Learning goals
- Review the concept of gravity
- Learn about the concept of air resistance
- Make hypotheses about how fast different objects land on the floor
- Test hypotheses and come to conclusions

STEAM subjects
- Science

Thinking skills
Remembering, applying, comparing, analyzing, concluding

Main language content
Balloon, building block, coin, cotton ball, die, eraser, feather, heavy, light, pencil, tissue
What goes up must come down
Which object will land first?
I think the (eraser) will land first.

OPENING

Circle time

Materials and preparation
- Visual schedule pictures

Say *hello* to students and invite them to sit in a circle. Show them the visual schedule pictures and explain what they are for. Say, *These pictures show our schedule for the day. Let's check them out!* Show all pictures, one at a time, and teach students the name of the subjects. Ask them to say what kind of things they may learn in these subjects and help them understand a little more about them.

> **Note to teachers**
> Call on a student to be the class helper of the day. Tell this student to help you with materials and other simple tasks throughout today's lesson.

Science - How do scientists work?

Materials and preparation
- A building block
- A sheet of paper

Tell students that good scientists always ask questions, observe, make a hypothesis, and test their hypothesis to check if they are right. Show them the sheet of paper and the building block and ask who can remember the motto of gravity (*what goes up must come down*). Ask them if they think that the two objects in your hand will land on the floor at the same time. Ask them why they think that. Tell students you are going to drop both objects at the same time and they have to observe very carefully. Ask them, *What happened? Which object landed first? Why do you think so?* Tell students they are going to form a hypothesis about what happened to the objects.
Write their ideas on the board and make sure to include the words *light* and *heavy* in the discussion. Write the hypothesis on the board: *heavy objects land first*.

42 STEAM

> **Note to teachers**
> The scientific method is a way to ask and answer scientific questions by making hypotheses and testing them with experiments. It consists of six basic steps: ask a question, make observations, form a hypothesis, test your hypothesis, analyze the data, and draw a conclusion.

ACTIVE LEARNING

Science - Which object will land first?

Materials and preparation
- Project Book page 39
- The following pair of objects:
  - a balloon (filled with air) and a coin
  - a bird feather and an eraser
  - a cotton ball and a die
  - a paper tissue and a pencil

Tell students to open their Project Book to page 39, go over the items on the page and elicit the names of the objects. Introduce the new language.
Tell students they will make hypotheses about which object will land first when they are released in the air. Ask everyone to say what they think. Then have them draw their hypotheses in the first box. After they have finished drawing their hypotheses, choose two students at a time and ask them to come to the front of the class. Give each student one object from the pair and tell them to drop the objects at the same time. The other students should watch to see which object lands first and check their charts to see if they guessed it correctly. Do the same with the other pairs of objects and check students' work.
At the end of the activity, students should draw a conclusion based on their observations. The idea is to teach students that the lighter object will take longer to land than the heavier one.
After the experiment is ready, have students draw in the second box which object landed first.

DIFFERENTIATED INSTRUCTION

BELOW LEVEL
Testing more objects

Materials and preparation
- Students' personal objects

Tell students to select two other objects that they have on them to test their hypotheses. Have students drop the objects and check which one landed first. Help them say, *(My pencil) landed first.*

ABOVE LEVEL

Materials and preparation
- Students' personal objects

Tell students to select four other objects that they have on them to test their hypotheses. Have students drop the objects and check which one landed first. Help them say, *(My pencil) landed first.*

CLOSING

Saying goodbye

Say *goodbye* to each student individually and ask them to say what their favorite part of the class was.

Learning goals
- Compare and contrast man-made garbage and natural residues
- Talk about the importance of not throwing garbage away
- Learn about different recyclable materials and the color codes used in recycling bins

STEAM subjects
- Science
- Math

Thinking skills
Remembering, comparing, analyzing, categorizing

Main language content
Dead flowers, glass, leaves, metal, plastic, paper, seeds, shells, recycle, throw away, recycling bins, trash

OPENING

Circle time

Materials and preparation
- Visual schedule pictures

Say *hello* to students and invite them to sit in a circle. Show them the visual schedule pictures and explain what they are for. Say, *These pictures show our schedule for the day. Let's check them out!* Show all pictures, one at a time, and teach students the name of the subjects. Ask them to say what kind of things they may learn in these subjects and help them understand a little more about them.

> **Note to teachers**
> You can print out pictures of students doing these activities and use them for the visual schedule.

Science - A nature walk

Tell students they are going to take a quick walk outside and that they are going to be explorers. Tell them they are going to collect a few things from the ground, but they cannot collect living flowers or animals. As you walk, show them what they can collect: dead flowers, twigs, leaves, dead insects, seeds, eggshells, anything that is on the ground and is from nature.

> **Note to teachers**
> If a yard walk is not possible, bring some dead flowers, dead leaves, twigs, eggshells, and other items from nature that decompose naturally.

ACTIVE LEARNING

Science - Our planet

Materials and preparation

- Items collected during the nature walk
- Recyclable items: glass bottles, plastic bottles, paper, soda cans, etc.

Return to the classroom and ask students to place their findings in the middle of the circle. Ask them what they think happens to these items after some time has passed. Explain that these items will become part of the soil and make it more fertile for other plants to grow. Ask them if they think the same happens for things we throw away. Explain that a plastic bag will take a long time to decompose and that is why it is important to recycle and to throw our garbage in the correct places.

Ask students what kinds of things they throw in the garbage can at home. Elicit items such as plastic bottles and bags, wrapping paper, foam trays, aluminum paper, cans, glass jars and bottles, etc. Ask students to imagine all these items are going somewhere. There is no "throwing away" — everything stays on our planet. Take students outside and show them recycling bins or bring pictures of these to class. Elicit the colors of the bins and the material each color represents.

Math - Let's help! Color. Count the items we can recycle.

Materials and preparation

- Colored pencils
- Markers
- Project Book page 41

Have students open their Project Book to page 41. Ask them what they see. Ask students a few questions about the picture: *Where are the people? What are they doing? What is the place like? Is it clean? Is it a nice place to play? Why not?* Tell them they are going to help the people in the park count the items that can be recycled.

Ask them to count the different items, complete the bins with the number of items, and then color the bins using the color you tell them to: green for organic waste, orange for paper, red for plastic, and blue for glass.

DIFFERENTIATED INSTRUCTION

More itens for the bins.

BELOW LEVEL

In trios, students think of one more item for each bin. Walk around and help them as needed. Write the new words on the board.

ABOVE LEVEL

In trios, students think of two more items for each bin. Walk around and help them as needed. Write the new words on the board.

CLOSING

Reflecting

Ask a few questions as a link to the following STEAM class students are going to have, *How can we reduce the amount of garbage we throw away.*

Saying goodbye

Say *goodbye* to students and have them say *goodbye* to you and to their classmates.

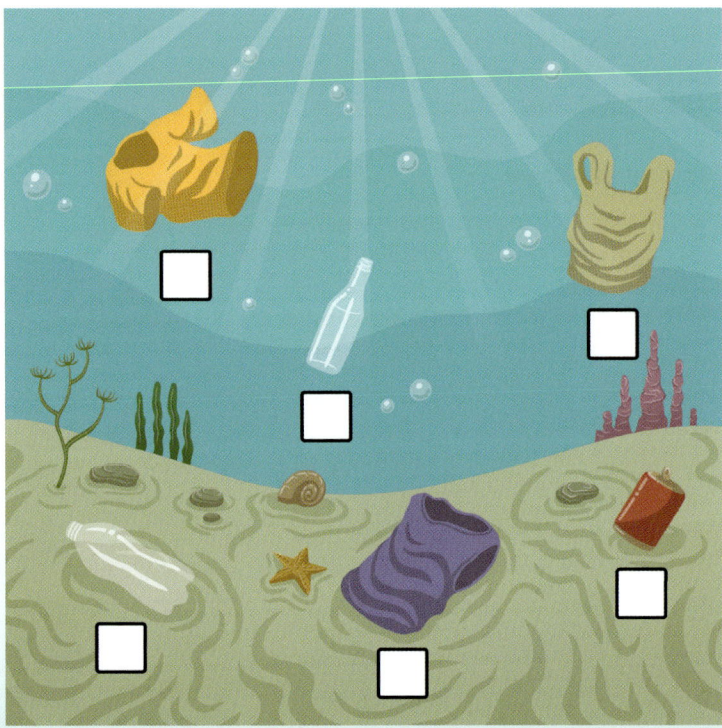

OPENING

Circle time

Materials and preparation
- Visual schedule pictures

Say *hello* to students and invite them to sit in a circle. Show them the visual schedule pictures and explain what they are for. Say, *These pictures show our schedule for the day. Let's check them out!* Show all pictures, one at a time, and teach students the name of the subjects. Ask them to say what kind of things they may learn in these subjects and help them understand a little more about them.

> **Note to teachers**
> Call on a student to be the class helper of the day. Tell this student to help you with materials and other simple tasks throughout today's lesson.

Science and arts – Let's take care of our planet!

Materials and preparation
- A large Styrofoam ball (about 15-30 cm wide)
- Masking tape
- Small pictures or cutouts (smaller than the Styrofoam ball) of different items: plastic bottle, glass bottle, diaper, cotton T-shirt, soda can, plastic bag, batteries
- Play dough (blue, brown, and green)

Ask students whether they can remember the types of recyclable materials they saw in the previous class. Show them the Styrofoam ball and tell them they are going to make planet Earth. Show students a few pictures of planet Earth and ask them what colors they see (green, blue for the oceans, white for the clouds). Place the ball in the middle of the circle and help students cover it using play dough. Help them with the green and brown parts in order to resemble the continents.
After it is ready, hand out the cutouts representing the trash and ask students to stick them around the planet. Tell them to imagine the planet full of garbage. Ask them what they can do to help the planet.

Learning goals
- Learn about the importance of practicing the three Rs
- Understand the impact our trash causes on the environment
- Sing a song about the three R's

STEAM subjects
- Science
- Math

Thinking skills
Remembering, applying, comparing, estimating, analyzing, concluding

Main language content
Reduce, reuse, recycle, planet, Earth, take care, protect, plastic, glass, metal, paper, batteries, diapers, T-shirts
What can we do to help our planet? How can we reuse/reduce/recycle our trash?

ACTIVE LEARNING

Science and math – How long until they are gone?

Materials and preparation

- Pictures/cutouts of different items: plastic bottle, glass bottle, diaper, cotton T-shirt, soda can, plastic bag, batteries
- Project Book page 43

Tell students that the items in the cutouts take a very long time to disappear. Write on the board the numbers that correspond to the time it takes for the items to decompose (see answer key below). Have them use the phrases *a really long time, a pretty long time, not a very long time* to refer to how long the item takes to decompose. Show students the cutouts one at a time and ask them to take a guess. Stick the cutouts next to the number, always asking students to take a guess first.

Ask students to open their Project Book to page 43 and complete the drawing with the number of years it takes for the items to be gone.

How long it takes to decompose:
- Glass Bottles – One Million Years
- Plastic Bottles – 450 years
- Disposable Diapers – 450 years
- Aluminum Cans – 80-200 years
- Plastic Bag – 10-20 years
- Cotton T-shirt – 5 months

> **Note to teachers**
> If you want to learn more about the topic, access https://www.ways2gogreenblog.com/2017/01/05/teaching-children-about-the-importance-of-recycling/; https://tjctransport.co.uk/blog/teaching-children-recycle/; (accessed on August 28, 2019).

Science – The three Rs

Materials and preparation

- Going green song (Earth Day song for kids about the 3 R's – Reduce, Reuse, and Recycle) available on YouTube

Talk to students about what the Three Rs stand for: *Reduce, Reuse,* and *Recycle*. Tell them they are going to listen to a song that shows people how we can do them. Play the video once and ask students to list the items mentioned in the song. Play it again and ask students to choose one thing they can do at home from the suggestions given in the song.

DIFFERENTIATED INSTRUCTION

BELOW LEVEL
Draw two items you use at home.

Materials and preparation

- Colored pencils or crayons
- Student's notebook

Ask students to draw two items they use at home and that can be reused.

ABOVE LEVEL

Ask students to draw a picture showing what they can do at home to help the environment.

CLOSING

Saying goodbye

As students to talk about the subjects they studied today, science and math. Ask them which one they like best and help them understand what subjects were related to each activity. Make sure everyone has a chance to give their opinion.
Say *goodbye* to each student individually and ask them to say what their favorite part of the class was.

Unit 5

Unit 6 How can you stay healthy?

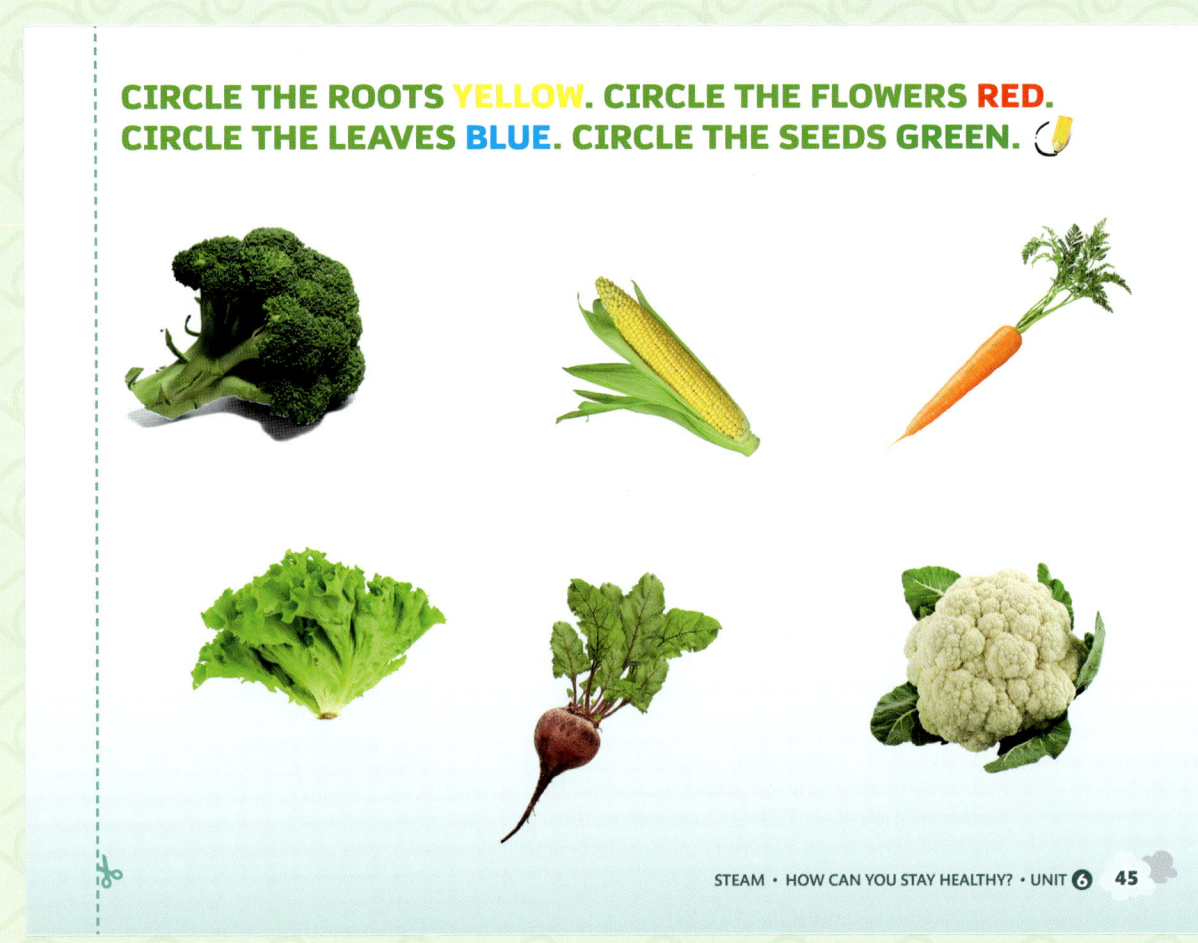

OPENING

Circle time

Materials and preparation

- Visual schedule pictures

Say *hello* to students and invite them to sit in a circle. Show them the visual schedule pictures and explain what they are for. Say, *These pictures show our schedule for the day. Let's check them out!* Show all pictures, one at a time, and teach students the name of the subjects. Ask them to say what kind of things they may learn in these subjects and help them understand a little more about them.

> **Note to teachers**
> You can print out pictures of students doing these activities and use them for the visual schedule.

Science and arts – What are the parts of a plant? What do plants need to survive?

Materials and preparation

- Brown string
- Colored pencils
- Cupcake liners
- Glue
- Green or brown plastic straws or pipe cleaners
- Green construction paper cut into the shape of leaves
- Poster paper or A3 sheet with the bottom colored in brown (to simulate the soil)
- Scissors
- Sunflower seeds (or any other type available)
- Straws or pipe cleaners

Ask students, *Who likes to eat fruits and vegetables?* and elicit some vegetables they like to eat. Remind them that the fruits and vegetables we eat come from trees and other plants. Tell students they are going to build a beautiful plant part by part. Show them the poster paper and draw their attention to the brown part. Tell

Learning goals

- Learn about the parts of a plant
- Learn about what plants need to survive
- Categorize vegetables according to the parts of a plant
- Understand the importance of eating different vegetables
- Plant seeds

STEAM subjects

- Science
- Arts
- Math

Thinking skills

Understanding, categorizing, comparing, analyzing.

Main language content

Flowers, leaves, plant, roots, seeds, soil, stem, survive, water
What parts of plants can we eat?
What part of the plant is this?

them that it is the soil, where the seeds begin to grow.
Then take a couple of seeds and ask a helper to glue them to the brown part. Explain that the seeds need to grow. Ask students what they think we need to do to make them grow (we need to water them). Ask another student to draw the drops of water using a blue colored pencil. Move on to the roots. Take the brown string and tell them that the plant will begin to grow. Place the pieces of string next to the seeds and ask another student to glue them to the paper. Use the straw or pipe cleaner to make the stem and explain that the stem is like a straw that sucks the nutrients from the soil and takes them to the leaves and the flowers. Ask another student to help you place the stem onto the paper. Next use the green paper for the leaves, doing the same procedure. Use the cupcake liner to make the flower and place more seeds in the middle of it, always asking for students' help every step of the way. When the flower is ready, ask students what else the plant needs to survive. Ask another student to draw the sun to show that plants need light. Finally tell students that plants also need care to grow. Ask students to sign the paper and hang the flower in the classroom. You may need to use L1 in some parts of this activity.

> **Note to teachers**
> If you have a large class, you might want to work with two flowers at the same time, so that more students get to help. Here is a picture for your reference https://www.teachjunkie.com/sciences/simple-3d-parts-of-a-plant-craft/ (accessed on August 28, 2019).

ACTIVE LEARNING

Science – What part of the plant is this?

Materials and preparation
- A stick of broccoli
- A carrot
- A piece of celery
- Some beans
- Some spinach leaves

Place the vegetables on a table or in the middle of the circle and ask students if they can name all of them. Remind them of the names of the parts of the plant they have just made and write them on the board (seeds, roots, stem, leaves, and flowers). Show students one item at a time and ask students what part of the plant they think it is. Tell them they are going to look at other food items we eat and decide what part of the plant they are.

Circle the roots yellow. Circle the flowers red. Circle the leaves blue. Circle the seeds green.

Materials and preparation
- Colored pencils
- Project Book page 45

Have students open their Project Book to page 45. Ask them to name the vegetables. Help them with vocabulary, if needed. Go over the color code with them and allow them to work on their own. At the end of the activity, ask students to tell you the ones they like to eat and tell the class.

DIFFERENTIATED INSTRUCTION

BELOW LEVEL
Name the parts of the food.

Materials and preparation
- Project Book page 45

Students point to different parts of the food items and name them. Allow them to refer to the plant they made in the beginning of the class.

ABOVE LEVEL

Ask students to label the parts of the food items according to the plant they made in the beginning of the class.

CLOSING

Expanding – Our class plant

Materials and preparation
- Small gardening tools
- Soil
- Some seeds
- Vase

Tell students they are going to have their own plant in the classroom. Show them what you are going to need to plant it and allow a few volunteers to help you. Keep the plant in the classroom and have students take turns watering it.

> **Note to teachers**
> It is important to choose a plant that is easy to take care of and does not require too much light. Here are some references to help you choose: https://www.teachstarter.com/us/blog/best-and-worst-indoor-plants-for-classrooms-us/ (accessed on August 29, 2019).

Saying goodbye

Materials and preparation
- Audio library – songs

Invite students to sing the *Goodbye song* (track 03) with you. Say *goodbye* to each of them and have them say *goodbye* back to you.

Unit 6

COLOR AND STICK THE CHARACTERS IN THE CORRECT ORDER.

STEAM • HOW CAN YOU STAY HEALTHY? • UNIT 47

Learning goals
- Listen to and understand a story
- Order the sequence of events using stickers
- Understand the principle of levers
- Make a simple lever to lift the enormous turnip

STEAM subjects
- Science
- Engineering
- Arts

Thinking skills
Remembering, applying, comparing, analyzing, concluding

Main language content
Words from the story: *boy cat, dad, dog, girl, mom, pulled, turnip*

OPENING

Circle time

Materials and preparation
- Visual schedule pictures

Say *hello* to students and invite them to sit in a circle. Show them the visual schedule pictures and explain what they are for. Say, *These pictures show our schedule for the day. Let's check them out!* Show all pictures, one at a time, and teach students the name of the subjects. Ask them to say what kind of things they may learn in these subjects and help them understand a little more about them.

> **Note to teachers**
> Call on a student to be the class helper of the day. Tell this student to help you with materials and other simple tasks throughout today's lesson.

Arts – Storytelling: *The enormous turnip*

Materials and preparation
- Any version of the story *The enormous turnip* (see suggestions)

Ask students what they remember from the previous STEAM class they had. Elicit the parts of the plant and ask them to give some examples of each part by drawing them on the board. Ask students if they have ever heard of the story of the enormous turnip. Remind them of what a turnip is and show them a picture or a real turnip. Use your version to tell students the story. If you do not have a book, choose one of the videos available and pause every time someone else comes to help pull the turnip. Make sure you build the sequence step by step:

Dad pulled the turnip. Mom pulled Dad who pulled the turnip. The boy pulled Mom, who pulled Dad, who pulled the turnip. The girl pulled the boy, who pulled Mom, who pulled Dad, who pulled the turnip. The dog pulled the girl... The cat pulled the dog, who pulled... The mouse pulled the cat, who pulled...

At the end of the story, ask students why they were able to pull up the turnip only when the mouse helped. Explain the moral of the story: even though the mouse was the smallest of them all, without its help they wouldn't have pulled the turnip up — every bit of help counts, no matter how small.

> **Note to teachers**
> There are a few versions of *The enormous turnip* available online. Make sure you choose one with both the son and the daughter in it.

ACTIVE LEARNING

Arts – Color and stick the characters in the correct order.

Materials and preparation
- Colored markers
- Project Book page 47
- Stickers

Lead students back to their seats and ask them to open their Project Book to page 47. Have them look at the template and tell them to color the turnip. Have students get some colored markers and find the stickers page. Invite them to color the stickers as they wish. Then have them take out the stickers. Tell them they have to order the characters according to the order they helped pull the turnip up.

Engineering – Building a lever to lift the turnip

Materials and preparation
- A large building block
- A ruler
- A turnip

After students have finished the activity, ask them if they think the turnip was heavy or light. They should conclude that, based on the size, the turnip was probably very heavy. Ask them to imagine how the family took the enormous turnip home, being so big and heavy. Explain that when we need to lift something very heavy we can use a lever. Use some school objects to show how it works: say that when you place a long bar (the ruler) onto a fulcrum (the building block), then place one end under the turnip, and apply force to the other end, you are making a lever to lift the turnip. Show students how it works and tell them that the force will be different according to the location of the fulcrum – the closer the fulcrum is to the object to be lifted, the easier it is to lift the item.

> **Note to teachers**
> Learn more about levers:
> https://learning-center.homesciencetools.com/article/how-to-make-a-lever-simple-machines-science-project/
> See some examples of simple levers:
> https://www.sciencebuddies.org/teacher-resources/lesson-plans/lifting-with-a-lever; https://inventorsoftomorrow.com/2016/10/12/levers-2/ (accessed on August 29, 2019)

DIFFERENTIATED INSTRUCTION

BELOW LEVEL
Draw the turnip.

Materials and preparation
- Colored pencils
- Sheets of paper

Ask students to draw the turnip being lifted by a lever.

ABOVE LEVEL

Materials and preparation
- Colored pencils
- Sheets of paper

Ask students to draw the turnip being lifted by a lever and think of materials that can be used to build that lever.

CLOSING

Saying goodbye

Have students share their drawings and exchange ideas on the materials that can be used to build that lever. Say *goodbye* to each student individually and ask them to say what their favorite part of the class was.

Learning goals
- Understand the difference between processed food items and more natural kinds of food
- Learn about food processing
- Make a food processing machine
- Explain the steps to use their food machine

STEAM subjects
- Science
- Technology

Thinking skills
Remembering, understanding, categorizing, evaluating, creating.

Main language content
My food machine makes (bread).
It turns (eggs) into (omelets).
First you put the (eggs) here.
Then you press the button/turn it on.
Finally, you get (an omelet).

OPENING

Circle time

Materials and preparation
- Visual schedule pictures

Say *hello* to students and invite them to sit in a circle. Show them the visual schedule pictures and explain what they are for. Say, *These pictures show our schedule for the day. Let's check them out!* Show all pictures, one at a time, and teach students the name of the subjects. Ask them to say what kind of things they may learn in these subjects and help them understand a little more about them.

> **Note to teachers**
> You can print out pictures of students doing these activities and use them for the visual schedule.

Science and technology – Understanding food processing

Materials and preparation
- Pictures/flashcards of the following: a hamburger, a jar of jam, a potato, baby food, berries, bread, cheese, chips, chocolate, cocoa (the fruit), corn, different vegetables, flour or wheat, a milk bottle, piece of meat, potato popcorn, tomato, tomato sauce

Place the pictures/flashcards in the middle of the circle. Elicit the names of the food items in the pictures and ask students what they like to eat. Introduce the words they don't know. Write all the words on the board. Then ask students to find a way to categorize the food items: *How would you group them together?* Allow them to create their own categories and handle the pictures or flashcards. Remind them that when we categorize things, we must have a system. Ask, *Why are you grouping particular things together? What do they have in common?* Ask students what their criteria was and tell them that you are going to categorize the food items into only two categories. Take the pictures of the jam and the berries and place them one in two different columns. Ask students if they can see why. Tell a volunteer to try with two other flashcards.

Help them through the process, the idea being to help them see that in one column you have the raw materials to make processed food items (in the second column). Explain that sometimes we can process food items at home and sometimes the food items are processed in a factory. Ask students for more examples of food items that are made from the raw materials in the pictures (juice, cookies, cakes, yogurt, canned vegetables, soup, etc.). Ask students to think about other examples of food items that are processed. Ask, *Are they always healthy? What other ingredients are added to processed food items?*

Note to teachers
Processed food items are part of our everyday diet. Ultra-processed food items, on the other hand, have many ingredients and substances that can be harmful to our health and should be avoided especially because of the excessive amount of sugar and salt in them. If you have time to go over this topic with the students, highlight that junk food is usually ultra-processed food (frozen French fries, frozen pizza and pasta dishes, store-bought cookies and chips, etc.).

ACTIVE LEARNING

Draw your food machine.
Materials and preparation
- Colored pencils
- Crayons
- Glue
- Markers
- Masking tape
- Old buttons and light switches
- Paint
- Recyclable materials, such as plastic bottles and containers, paper boxes, cartons, cans, etc.

As a class, tell students to imagine they could build a machine that can make food. Ask them what they would like to make. Give some examples: *I would like to have a machine that turns eggs into omelets. You put the eggs into the machine, press a button, and the omelet comes out nice and warm.* Ask students what they would like to make and how they would build their machines. Lead them to their tables/desks and show them the materials. They should work on building their food machines so that later they can "show" how they work.

Encourage students to present their machines. Encourage them to use the prompts below:

My food machine makes _____.
It turns _____ into _____.
First you put the _____ here.
Then you press the button/turn it on.
Finally, you get _____.

Create a food machine.
Materials and preparation
- Colored pencils
- Project Book page 49

Lead students back to their seats and tell them to open their Project Book to page 49. They should use it to make a drawing of their invention in action.

DIFFERENTIATED INSTRUCTION

BELOW LEVEL
Present a food machine.
Materials and preparation
- Project Book page 49

In trios, students choose one of the food machines and practice presenting it using the prompts used before.

ABOVE LEVEL
Materials and preparation
- Project Book page 49

In pairs, students practice presenting each other's food machine.

CLOSING

Reflecting
Ask students to think of their favorite natural food items and help the class list them. Ask, *Are any of them unhealthy?* The idea is to help them notice that the less food items are processed, the healthier they will be.

Saying goodbye
Say *goodbye* to students and have them say *goodbye* to you and to their classmates.

Learning goals
- List and categorize food items in alphabetical order.
- Create a name acrostic using the food items listed.
- Present the acrostics to the class.

STEAM subjects
- Arts
- Math

Thinking skills
Remembering, classifying, evaluating, creating

Main language content
Do you like (fries)?
What are the food items with the letters of your name?
(A) is for (apple).
What can we do to help the planet? How can we reuse/reduce/recycle our trash?

OPENING

Circle time

Materials and preparation
- Visual schedule pictures

Say *hello* to students and invite them to sit in a circle. Show them the visual schedule pictures and explain what they are for. Say, *These pictures show our schedule for the day. Let's check it out!* Show all pictures, one at a time, and teach students the name of the subjects. Ask them to say what kind of things they may learn in these subjects and help them understand a little more about them.

Note to teachers
Call out a student to be the class helper of the day. Tell this student to help you with materials and other simple tasks throughout today's lesson.

Math – Food alphabet

Materials and preparation
- Alphabet set: letters A-F
- Labeled pictures of different food items and drinks (suggestions: apple, bread, carrot, doughnut, egg, fries)

Display the alphabet letters and the pictures of food/drink items in the circle. Show students the food items, elicit the names they already know, teach the ones they do not know yet, and have them repeat. Ask students whether they are able to classify the food items according to the letter they begin with. Allow students some time to work and make sure to reinforce the names of the food items as they do it. When students finish categorizing the pictures, make sure to keep them in alphabetical order somewhere visible to the students.

ACTIVE LEARNING

Naming food items

Lead students back to their seats. Ask students to check the food item(s) listed under the first letter of their names. Ask, *Do you like any of these food items? How many of them have you tried?* Write the letters of your first name on the board. Ask students to help you make an acrostic using only names of food and drink items, or words that are related to food. Ask the help of volunteers for every letter of your name. Explain that what you just did is called a *name acrostic*, which is a kind of poem that you can do, for example, out of a person's name.

Arts and math – Create a delicious acrostic.

Materials and preparation

- Labeled pictures of food items (in order)
- Project Book Page 51

Tell students to open their Project Book to page 51. Explain they are going to do the same thing with their names — create an acrostic. Ask them to use the food and drink items listed previously. They can also illustrate their poems by drawing the food and drink items they use. Exemplify: *My name is (Alice) and I eat bananas and cereal: A, B, C!*
Monitor their work and help students spell words if necessary.
When all students have finished, invite them to present their poems to the class.

DIFFERENTIATED INSTRUCTION

BELOW LEVEL
Let's create!

Materials and preparation
- Pencil
- Sheets of paper (one per student)

Ask students to create another acrostic with the name of their school. Allow them to do this activity in pairs.

ABOVE LEVEL

Do the procedures explained in *Below level*, but have pairs of students make longer acrostics.

CLOSING

Saying goodbye

Have students say the part of the class they liked most. Say *goodbye* to students and have them say *goodbye* to you and to their classmates.

Unit 7 How can you take care of animals?

Learning goals
- Classify animals according to their habitats
- Recognize kinds of animals
- Classify animals into wild or domestic

STEAM subjects
- Science
- Arts
- Math

Thinking skills
Recognizing, classifying, sharing information

Main language content
Animals: *cat, crocodile, duck, eagle, fish, hamster, lion, monkey, octopus, rabbit*

OPENING

Circle time

Materials and preparation
- Visual schedule pictures

Say *hello* to students and invite them to sit in a circle. Show them the visual schedule pictures and explain what they are for. Say, *These pictures show our schedule for the day. Let's check them out!* Show all pictures, one at a time, and teach students the name of the subjects. Ask them to say what kind of things they may learn in these subjects and help them understand a little more about them.

> **Note to teachers**
> You can print out pictures of students doing these activities and use them for the visual schedule.

Science and math – Recognizing habitats and classifying animals

Materials and preparation
- Pictures of animals studied in Unit 7, including octopus, crocodile, duck, and fish
- Three thin strips of paper to be used as headers to the spaces in the diagram: strip 1: a picture of a park and the word *land*; strip 2: a picture of a lake and the word *water*; strip 3: a picture of a park, a picture of a lake and the words *land* and *water*
- Two hula-hoops

In the circle on the floor, assemble the hula-hoops as a Venn diagram, with an intersection. Place the headers on top of each empty space: *land* on the left side, *water* on the right side, and *land and water* in the intersection. Take one picture of a land animal and ask, *What animal is this?* Once students answer correctly, ask, *Where do (ducks) live: on land, in the water or on land and in the water?* Point to the words in the headers as you say them. Elicit the answer from students and say, *(Ducks) live on land* and have students repeat. Then place the picture in the correct space. Take the picture of an aquatic animal and do the same. Then take the picture of the duck, ask for the name of the animal and then ask, *Where do the ducks live?* Elicit the answer and help if necessary. Proceed like this until students have identified and classified all the pictures.

ACTIVE LEARNING

Math – classifying animals

Materials and preparation

- Brown paper bags
- Masking tape
- Pictures of wild and domestic animals on cardboard paper with strings or double-sided tape on the back (for students to hang or glue the pictures on the board) – one set of pictures for each group of students (prepared by you before class starts)

Before class, place the sets of pictures in brown paper bags. Do not include pictures of chimpanzees, eagles, lions, hamsters, rabbits, or cats. Organize students into small groups. Divide the board into as many columns as you have groups and then number the columns. Divide each column into two parts and name the parts *domestic* and *wild*. Place a chair in front of each column, allowing some room between the board and the chairs so students can move around. Tell students that this is a competition. Ask each group to form a line behind one of the chairs. Point to the numbers on the board and say to the first group, *You are group one*. Go to the next group and say, *You are group two*. Go on until all groups know their numbers. Place one brown paper bag with pictures on each chair. Explain that the first student in each line will take a picture from the brown bag, place it in the correct place on the board, and go to the end of their groups' line. They are not supposed to look inside the bag; they must work with the picture they get. When the first student is back in their group, the second student takes a picture from the bag and does the same. This procedure is to be repeated until one group places its last picture on the board, and this group is the winner. You may want to bring a token to give the winning group. If time allows, let the other groups finish their task, too; then you can assign second and third places.

Note to teachers

Classifying and sorting is important in early age because they are the foundation for more complex mathematical thinking. If possible, bring in a mystery box or a box of surprises with different classifications of objects inside and have students classify the objects collaboratively. Classification can include heavy and light, long and short, man-made and natural, etc.

Science, arts, and math – Color the domestic animals.

Materials and preparation

- Colored pencils
- Project Book page 53

Lead students to their desks and have students open their Project Book to page 53. Tell students that they are to color only the domestic animals. Instruct them to use realistic colors as much as possible and to write the name of each animal in the white strip on top of each illustration. Tell them not to cut out the illustrations for now. In pairs, students tell each other some characteristics of the animals they colored. For example, *A cat has fur, a tail and four legs*. If time allows, have them say some characteristics of the wild animals as well. Keep their work for next class.

DIFFERENTIATED INSTRUCTION

BELOW LEVEL
Science – Sharing information about animals

In pairs, students talk about two animals. One student says the name of an animal and asks, *Where do (animals) live? Are they wild or domestic?* The other student answers both questions. When the first student has answered correctly, it is their turn to ask the questions so the first one will answer.

ABOVE LEVEL

In pairs, students talk about two animals. One student say the name of an animal and asks, *Where do (animals) live? Are they wild or domestic? What do (animals) eat?* The other student answers all three questions. When the first student has answered correctly, it is their turn to ask the questions so the first one will answer.

CLOSING

Saying goodbye

Say *goodbye* to each student individually and ask them to say what their favorite part of the class was. Say, *See you tomorrow* and have them say it back to you.

GLUE DOMESTIC ANIMALS IN THE YARD.

STEAM • HOW CAN YOU TAKE CARE OF ANIMALS? • UNIT 7   55

Learning goals
- Learn about sequencing and practice it
- Identify animals by their characteristics
- Place domestic animals in their usual habitat

STEAM subjects
- Science
- Arts
- Math

Thinking skills
Identifying, classifying, compiling, inferring

Main language content
Animals: *bird, cat, dog, fish, lion, mouse*
Animal characteristics: *big, domestic, feathers, fur, small, wild*

OPENING

Circle time
Materials and preparation
- Visual schedule pictures

Say *hello* to students and invite them to sit in a circle. Show them the visual schedule pictures and explain what they are for. Say, *These pictures show our schedule for the day. Let's check them out!* Show all pictures, one at a time, and teach students the name of the subjects. Ask them to say what kind of things they may learn in these subjects and help them understand a little more about them.

> **Note to teachers**
> Call on a student to be the class helper of the day. Tell this student to help you with materials and other simple tasks throughout today's lesson.

Science and arts – Play the *Chain game*.
Materials and preparation
- Flashcards: *bird, cat, dog, fish, lion, mouse*

Tell students they are going to play a chain game. Place the flashcards on your table and invite volunteers to come to the front of the class, take a flashcard, and hold it facing their classmates. Repeat until all flashcards are with a student and they are holding it facing their classmates.
Have the rest of the class say the words in order. Then take one student from the group and leave that space blank. Ask students to say all the flashcards again and try to remember the one missing to include in the chain. Repeat with other flashcards. You may also remove more than one card.

ACTIVE LEARNING

Science – Recognizing animal characteristics

Materials and preparation

- Animal pictures – one set of five pictures for each pair of students
- A small box for each pair of students

Before class, set aside pictures of different animals, making sure to include only animals that students are familiar with. Tell students you will be playing an animal guessing game. Take one of the sets of pictures and show them to the class. Have students say the name of each animal before you move on to the next. Demonstrate the procedure by inviting a volunteer and having them come to the front of the class. The student chooses one of the pictures and shows it to the class, but not to you, and then puts it back with the other pictures. Tell them you will ask them questions to try to find out what it is. Tell your volunteer to sit back down. Ask the class simple questions about the animal and have them answer. You can ask, *Does it have fur? Does it have feathers? Does it eat fruit? Does it eat other animals? Is it big? Is it small? Is it domestic? Is it wild? How many legs does it have?* Every time you ask a question, write the keyword (*fur, fruit, wild*) on the board and eliminate the picture of all animals that do not fit that description. For example, if they say that the animal has fur, tell them, *It has fur, so it can't be the parrot. The parrot is out of the game* – and put that picture in the box. Go on asking questions until you find out what animal your volunteer chose – it will be the last remaining picture. Organize students into pairs, hand out the sets of pictures and a box, and let them play. Walk around the classroom assessing their performance and helping whenever needed. Keep going until everyone has guessed the animals correctly.

Science, arts, and math – Glue domestic animals in the yard.

Materials and preparation

- Colored pencils
- Masking tape or glue
- Project Book page 53 from previous class
- Project Book page 55
- Scissors

Lead students to their desks. Have them open their Project Book to page 53, the one they colored during the previous class. Ask them to cut out the images they colored and teach them how to fold the black stripe backwards to make the illustration stand up. Have them open their Project Book to page 55 and cut the landscape out. Tell students to glue or tape the black stripe on the domestic animals anywhere they want in the landscape.

DIFFERENTIATED INSTRUCTION

BELOW LEVEL
Science and arts – Sharing information about animals

Materials and preparation

- Sheets of paper – one for each student

Give each pair of students a sheet of paper. Students choose one animal to draw and color. On the same paper, they make a list of three things they know about that animal. For example, they write *fur, wild, small*.

ABOVE LEVEL

Give each pair of students a sheet of paper. Students choose one animal to draw and color. On the same paper, they make a list of everything they know about that animal. For example, they write *fur, wild, land, small, carnivorous*.

CLOSING

Saying goodbye

Materials and preparation

- Audio library - songs

Invite students to sing the *Goodbye song* (track 03) before they leave. Say *goodbye* to each student individually and ask them to say *goodbye* back to you.

MATCH EACH ANIMAL WITH WHAT IT NEEDS.

Learning goals
- Recognize the shapes of different animals
- Use a tangram
- Identify the needs of an animal

STEAM subjects
- Science
- Arts
- Math

Thinking skills
Recognizing, classifying, discussing

Main language content
Animals: *bird, cat, dog, fish, parrot*
Animal characteristics: *big, feathers, fur, small, whiskers*

OPENING

Circle time

Materials and preparation
- Visual schedule pictures

Say *hello* to students and invite them to sit in a circle. Show them the visual schedule pictures and explain what they are for. Say, *These pictures show our schedule for the day. Let's check them out!* Show all pictures, one at a time, and teach students the name of the subjects. Ask them to say what kind of things they may learn in these subjects and help them understand a little more about them.

> **Note to teachers**
> You can print out pictures of students doing these activities and use them for the visual schedule.

Science – Recognizing animals' needs

Materials and preparation
- Pictures of a cat, a bird, a fish, and a dog

Tell students that you are going to talk about how to care for pets. Explain that their pets need different things to stay healthy and happy, and just like how they can't take care of themselves without help from their families, their pets also can't take care of themselves without their owners. On the board, place pictures of a cat, a bird, a fish, and a dog. Have students name each animal as you place them. Explain that you are going to read them four riddles and they have to try to answer them. Make sure everybody understands what a riddle is. Read them the first riddle. When the students get the answer right, circle the corresponding picture on the board. If time allows, discuss what other pets exist and what they need from their owners.

Riddle 1: *Put me in cool water. Feed me. What am I?*
Riddle 2: *Clean my cage. Give me seeds to eat. Give me space to fly. What am I?*
Riddle 3: *Brush me. Feed me. Take me for walks. What am I?*
Riddle 4: *Clean my litter box. Give me food and water. Keep me inside the house. What am I?*

ACTIVE LEARNING

Arts and math – Drawing and recognizing the shapes of different animals using a tangram

Materials and preparation

- Cardboard tangram pieces – one set for each student (prepared by you before class starts)
- Drawing paper (five pieces per pair of students)
- Pencils, markers, or crayons

Before class, prepare a set of tangram pieces per pair of student, cutting the pieces out of cardboard. Also, look online for reference pictures of a tangram cat, fish, rabbit, bird, and turtle.
Tell students you are going to play with a tangram. Ask if they have played with one before. Show students each piece of the tangram and have them name each shape before you move on to the next. Hand out a tangram set and five pieces of paper to each student. Tell students that you are going to draw the pieces on the board and they have to replicate your drawing with their tangrams on top of the paper. Following a reference picture, draw a tangram cat on the board and allow some time for students to put theirs together. Ask, *What animal did we make?* Have pairs help each other in tracing around the tangram to outline their cat. Repeat the procedure for the other animals. Once all the animals are outlined on paper, tell students to finish the drawings by adding things like eyes, noses, whiskers, and whatever else they need to make their animals complete.

> **Note to teachers**
> Before you assign the activity, tell students what a tangram is (a special kind of puzzle made of different geometric shapes; it forms many different pictures depending on how the pieces are arranged).

Science and math – Match each animal with what it needs

Materials and preparation

- Colored pencils
- Project Book page 57

Tell students that you will be talking about how to take care of pets. Introduce the topic by saying, *Raise your hand if you have pets at home*. Count the students who raised their hands and write down the number of students who have pets on the board. Underneath it, write the word *pets*. Ask students to raise their hand if they have a dog. Count them and write down the number of students who raised their hands and the word *dogs*. Do the same for cats, birds, fish, and other animals, labeling the numbers accordingly (*cats, birds, fish*, etc.). Ask, *Are there more people who have dogs or cats? Cats or birds?* and so on. Ask, *How many dogs are there?* and have them say the total amount. Do the same for the other animals. Together, you and the class will come to a conclusion about the most common pets. Ask, *Which is the most popular animal in this classroom?* Point to all the animals written on the board and ask, *Do all animals have the same needs?* Elicit the answer and then allow a minute or two for discussion. Finally point out that, although their pets eat different food and live in different environments, they all need food, water, and to be clean and safe. They also need affection.
Explain that animals can't use words to communicate what they need. Therefore, the people responsible for them need to pay close attention to make sure their animals are healthy and happy. Ask, *Do you help take care of your pet? How?* Enforce the idea that everyone in the house is responsible for the wellbeing of a pet, including children. Tell students to turn to Project Book page 57 and ask them to name the animals they see. Explain that the animals in the left column need their help and that they should trace a line connecting each animal to what it needs.

DIFFERENTIATED INSTRUCTION

BELOW LEVEL
Math – Drawing and recognizing the shapes of different animals using a tangram

Materials and preparation

- Cardboard tangram pieces – one set for each pair of students (same pieces used in previous activity)

Organize students into pairs. Have one of them remake one of the tangram animals from the lesson while their partner tries to guess what it is. Then have students switch roles.

ABOVE LEVEL

Organize students into pairs. Have one of them use their tangram to make a different animal that wasn't in the lesson, while their classmate tries to guess what it is. Then have students switch roles.

CLOSING

Saying goodbye

Materials and preparation

- Audio library - songs

Sing the *Goodbye song* (track 03) and have students move the way they like. Have the puppet start and students continue. Encourage everybody to participate.

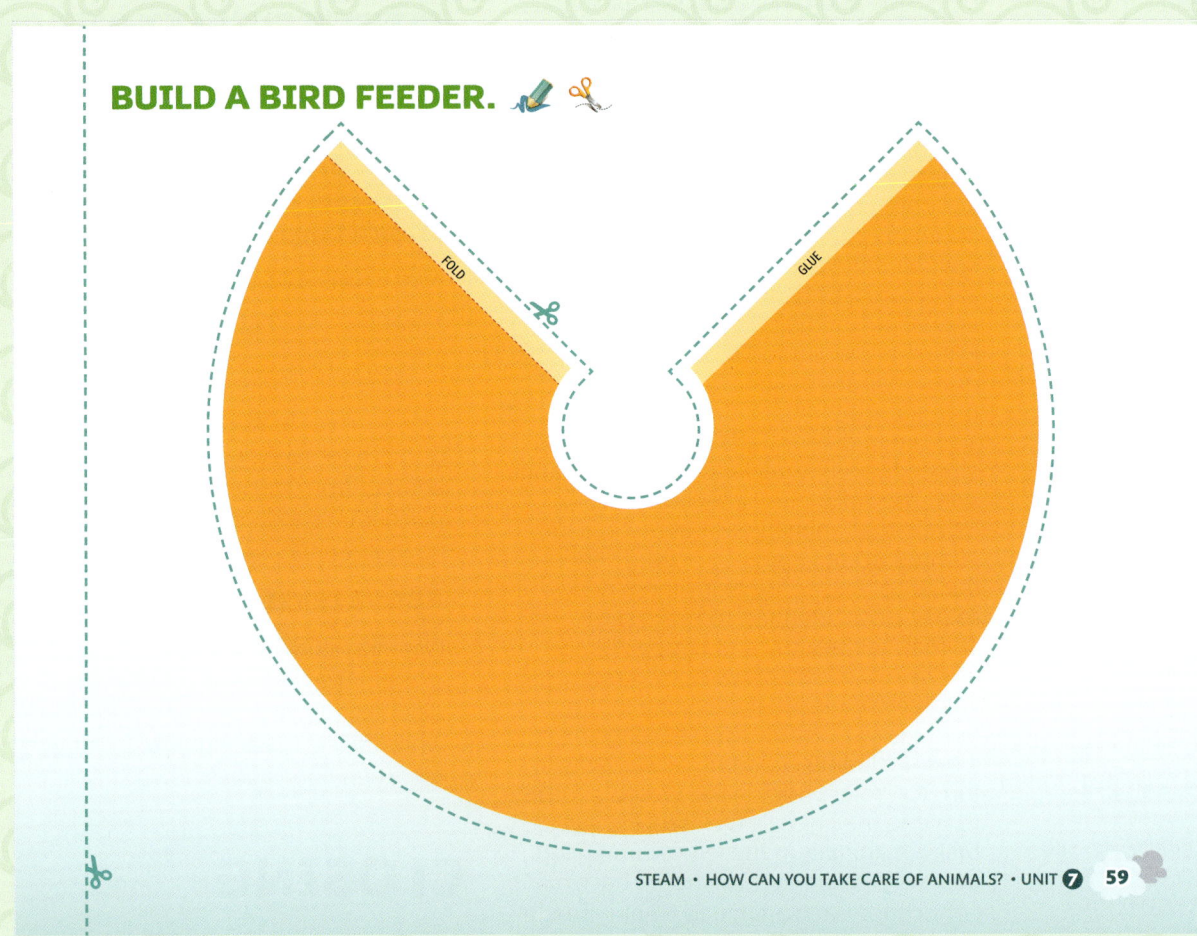

BUILD A BIRD FEEDER.

STEAM • HOW CAN YOU TAKE CARE OF ANIMALS? • UNIT 7   59

Learning goals
- Recall animal characteristics
- Classify objects
- Discuss animal care

STEAM subjects
- Science
- Engineering
- Arts
- Math

Thinking skills
Identifying, classifying, constructing, demonstrating, recalling, discussing

Main language content
Animals: *bird, eagle, fish, penguin, lion, zebra*
Animal characteristics: *big, domestic, fast, feathers, fur, long (neck), short (legs), slow, small, spot, stripe, wild*
Animal food: *fish, leaves, meat*

OPENING

Circle time

Materials and preparation
- Visual schedule pictures

Say *hello* to students and invite them to sit in a circle. Show them the visual schedule pictures and explain what they are for. Say, *These pictures show our schedule for the day. Let's check them out!* Show all pictures, one at a time, and teach students the name of the subjects. Ask them to say what kind of things they may learn in these subjects and help them understand a little more about them.

> **Note to teachers**
> Call on a student to be the class helper of the day. Tell this student to help you with materials and other simple tasks throughout today's lesson.

Science – Recalling animal characteristics

Materials and preparation
- Flashcards or pictures of animals: *bird, eagle, fish, penguin, lion, zebra*

Make a pile of flashcards face down in the middle of the circle. Organize students into groups. Explain that you are going to play a modified *lightning round*. You are going to show pictures of animals and ask short and fast questions to a group – for example, *Fruit or other animals?*, meaning *What does this animal eat, fruit or other animals?* Students in that group are supposed to answer the question very fast – for example, *Fruit*. If it takes more than five seconds for the group to answer correctly, the next group can answer the question. Model the activity once, helping a volunteer ask very fast, then proceed to the activity. Some of the many questions you may ask are:

Wild or domestic?   *Water or land?*
Fish or leaves?   *Big or small?*
Long neck or short neck? *Fast or slow?*
Four legs or two legs?   *Bird or fish? (for penguins only)*
Africa or Brazil?   *Spots or stripes?*

ACTIVE LEARNING

Science and math – Classifying objects and taking care of animals

Materials and preparation
- Assorted objects animals need and don't need – make sure to include a doctor doll or picture, medicine, food items, water, and a picture of animals receiving hugs from a person
- Bag
- Two thin strips of paper to be used as headers: strip 1: the word *yes*; strip 2: the word *no*

Prepare a bag of assorted objects before class. Make sure you choose mostly objects they are familiar with. Use a colored bag so that students can't see what is inside. Place the headers at a distance on the floor to make two columns – *yes* and *no*. Ask, *What makes an animal happy? How do you take care of your pet?* Elicit some ideas and write the answers on the board.
Take one object from the bag and ask, *What is this?* Help with vocabulary as needed. Ask, *Do animals need this to live?* Place the object in the correct column. Repeat the procedure with another object. Then take all the objects out of the bag and ask students to place them in the correct column. When they are done, ask students if the objects in column *yes* are enough to make an animal happy. Then ask, *What else does an animal need?* Allow students to share their ideas.

> **Note to teachers**
> Animals need preventive measures as much as humans do. Taking the pet to a vet is not only the owner's obligation, but also one of the most important ways of taking good care of the pet and ensuring they have a long, healthy, happy life.

Science, engineering, and arts – Build a bird feeder.

Materials and preparation
- Adhesive tape or glue
- Bird seed
- Colorful paper
- Disposable cups
- Markers
- Milk or juice cartons – one for each student (prepared by you before class starts)
- Pencils – one for each student (brand new ones, unsharpened)
- Project Book page 59
- Scissors
- Tape or glue

Before class, prepare the cartons, one for each student. First, wash them thoroughly. Then, on one of the sides, cut a hole (around 6 cm x 6 cm) in the shape of a circle or a square. The hole should be about 5cm above the bottom of the carton. Measurements do not need to be exact. Also, cut the colorful paper to a size big enough to wrap it around the carton. Ask students, *What do birds eat?* Allow time for guesses. Explain to them that while some big birds are carnivores, the small ones eat seed and fruit. Hand students the cartons, colorful paper, scissors, and tape or glue. Tell them they are going to build a bird feeder. Instruct them to wrap the colorful paper around the carton and glue or tape it in place. Help as necessary. Then help them cut out a big hole in the paper so it lines up with the hole in the box. Hand students the markers and have them decorate their cartons however they want to. While they decorate their cartons, walk around and use a sharpened pencil to poke a hole in each carton, underneath the big hole, to make it easier for students to insert the pencil that will be the perch for the birds. Make sure the pencil doesn't go through the carton. Then have students insert the new pencil in the small hole until it reaches the other side of the box. Explain that this will be the perch and that birds will use it to stand on while they eat.
Have students open their Project Book to page 59, cut out the funnel shape, and roll it into the shape of a proper funnel. Let them decorate the funnel, if time allows. Help them secure it with tape or glue. Explain to them that it will make it easier to pour the seed into the bird feeder. Distribute the bird seed into disposable cups for easier handling and give one to each student. Demonstrate how to pour the seed into the carton through the funnel, then have them do it themselves. Provide assistance where needed. There should be enough seed in each carton to either cover the pencil or stop just short of it. Tell students to take the bird feeder home and set it on a window so that birds can come and have a snack. Encourage them to share the activity with their families and take pictures if they see a bird eating from the feeder they made.

> **Note to teachers**
> Tell students they should keep the feeder clean so that birds won't get sick due to bacteria and other harmful threats.

> **Note to teachers**
> For reference and ideas on how to decorate the *milk carton bird feeder*, search the Internet.

DIFFERENTIATED INSTRUCTION

BELOW LEVEL
This is my bird feeder.

Materials and preparation
- Students' bird feeders

Ask students to share their bird feeders with the closest classmate and say, *This is my bird feeder.*

ABOVE LEVEL

Ask students to share their bird feeders with their classmate and say, *This is my bird feeder. Small birds eat seeds. I'll set this feeder on a window. Birds will have a snack.*

> **Note to teachers**
> Model with a student's bird feeder before you assign the task. Write the sentences on the board for students' reference.

CLOSING

Saying goodbye

Say *goodbye* to students and encourage them to say *goodbye* to you.

Unit 8 What is your favorite place in town?

CIRCLE YOUR FAVORITE PLACE IN TOWN.
THEN CIRCLE YOUR PARENTS' FAVORITE PLACES IN TOWN.

STEAM • WHAT IS YOUR FAVORITE PLACE IN TOWN? • UNIT 8   61

Learning goals
- Recognize different places in town
- Demonstrate a preference towards specific places
- Deduce answers based on simple clues

STEAM subjects
- Science
- Arts
- Math

Thinking skills
Recognizing, classifying, sharing information

Main language content
Places in town: *grocery store, hospital, library, mall, school*

OPENING

Circle time

Materials and preparation
- Visual schedule pictures

Say *hello* to students and invite them to sit in a circle. Show them the visual schedule pictures and explain what they are for. Say, *These pictures show our schedule for the day. Let's check them out!* Show all pictures, one at a time, and teach students the name of the subjects. Ask them to say what kind of things they may learn in these subjects and help them understand a little more about them.

> **Note to teachers**
> You can print out pictures of students doing these activities and use them for the visual schedule.

Science and arts – Say a rhyme.

Materials and preparation
- Picture of a supermarket (showing food) and toys in a toy store

Tell students they are going to help you identify where you can go in your town to buy things, but this will be done by rhyming. Teach them the rhyme. Use pictures the first time you say the rhyme.
T: *I want to buy a present for my friends. They are boys.*
S: *You can buy toys.*
T: *When my friend is hungry, she gets in a bad mood.*
S: *You can get her food.*

64 STEAM

ACTIVE LEARNING

Arts and math – Circle your favorite place in town. Then circle your parents' favorite places in town.

Materials and preparation
- Pencils or crayons
- Project Book page 61

Tell students to open their books to page 61 of the Project Book and pay close attention to what they see. Ask, *What places do you see?* and help them name the places one by one. As they do, write the names of the places on the board. Then tell students that you will find out what the best place in town is. Ask them to guess the places in the picture and circle the place they like the best. Then, with a different color, they should circle the place that their parents like the best. Allow time for students to do the activity. Once they are finished, choose one of the places on the board and ask students to raise their hands if they chose it as their favorite. Count the raised hands and write down the number next to the correct name on the board. Continue this process until you have the numbers for students' favorite places and their parents' favorite places. Finally ask, *Which of the places got the most votes from children? Which of them got the most votes from adults?*. Draw a star next to the names of the winning places.

Science – Making deductions based on clues

Materials and preparation
- A box full of candies or other small treats
- Double-sided tape
- Small envelopes (8)
- Small sheets of paper or index cards (8)

Before class, prepare the clues by writing *school, supermarket, shopping mall, bakery, drugstore, park, library,* and *bank* on the back of the envelopes. Write the same words (except for *school*) on small sheets of paper or index cards and put each one in an envelope with the previous word written on it (for example, the envelope that says *school* should contain the paper that says *supermarket*; the *supermarket* envelope should contain the *shopping mall* paper, and so on, until the last one leads to the *bank* envelope). On the last piece of paper, draw a key, and put it in the *bank* envelope. Finally, take a shoebox, fill it with candy or other small treats, and draw a keyhole on the front of the box. Tell students that they will be participating in a scavenger hunt together. First, attach the envelopes to the board with double-sided tape, either lined up randomly or scattered around the board. Then, show the box and say, *We need to find the key to open our treasure chest. There are clues in these envelopes to help us find it. Where are we now?* Students are supposed to answer, *At school.* Open the envelope with the word *school* on it and take out the clue. Instead of telling students the name of the place, give them clues so they can guess it themselves. For example, if the word inside the envelope is *supermarket*, you can say, *It is a place where you can buy food and groceries, It is a large building.* Once they correctly guess *supermarket*, open the *supermarket* envelope to retrieve the next clue. Keep following the same procedure until you reach the last envelope. Then, show students the key, announcing that they have solved the mystery. Finally, open the box and pass around the candy or treats to celebrate.

DIFFERENTIATED INSTRUCTION

BELOW LEVEL
Talking about likes and dislikes

Materials and preparation
- Pencils
- Project book page 61

In pairs, students look at the pictures in their books again and ask each other questions about their personal likes and dislikes. They ask questions like *Do you like going to the mall?* Then tell students to draw their partner smiling next to their favorite place and frowning next to their least favorite.

ABOVE LEVEL

In pairs, students look at the pictures in their books again and ask each other questions about their personal likes and dislikes. They ask questions like *Do you like going to the mall?* Then tell students to draw their partner smiling next to their favorite place and frowning next to their least favorite. After that, each student says one short sentence about their partner's personal opinions, for example, *John likes to go to school.*

CLOSING

Saying goodbye

Say *goodbye* to students and encourage them to say *goodbye* to you.

> **Note to teachers**
> Before saying goodbye, tell students to bring scrap materials for next class. Remember to write a note for parents as well.

DRAW YOUR FAVORITE PLACE IN TOWN AND GLUE IT.

STEAM • WHAT IS YOUR FAVORITE PLACE IN TOWN? • UNIT 8 63

Learning goals
- Infer places from context
- Describe places and what they do
- Share personal information

STEAM subjects
- Science
- Engineering

Thinking skills
Recalling, identifying, inferring, recognizing, describing, constructing

Main language content
Places in town: *drugstore, mall, park, restaurant, school, supermarket, toy store*

OPENING

Circle time

Materials and preparation
- Visual schedule pictures

Say *hello* to students and invite them to sit in a circle. Show them the visual schedule pictures and explain what they are for. Say, *These pictures show our schedule for the day. Let's check them out!* Show all pictures, one at a time, and teach students the name of the subjects. Ask them to say what kind of things they may learn in these subjects and help them understand a little more about them.

> **Note to teachers**
> Call on a student to be the class helper of the day. Tell this student to help you with materials and other simple tasks throughout today's lesson.

Science – Making deductions based on clues

Materials and preparation
- Brown bag
- Set of pictures of people inside places (prepared by you before class starts)
- Set of pictures of places in town (prepared by you before class starts)

Before class, prepare two sets of pictures. For the first set, select pictures of people inside some places in town, but we cannot see what place it is – students will find it out by analyzing what the people are doing. For example, choose a picture of a couple buying medicine in a drugstore. Select at least five pictures in five different places. Put these pictures in a brown bag and name it *people*. For the second set of pictures, select the front view of all the places where the people in the first set are in the pictures (drugstore, for example). Put this set of pictures in another brown bag and name it *places*.

Ask students to tell you the places in town they can remember. Write their contributions on the board. Take a picture from the *people* set and place it in the middle of the circle.

Ask students, *What is this person doing?* Elicit answers. Ask, *Where is the person?* Let students make guesses until they get their answer right. Then ask, *How do you know?* Elicit answers and help with vocabulary and grammar if necessary. Take the corresponding picture from the *places* bag and place it next to the other people. Take another picture from the *people* bag and follow the same steps. Repeat this procedure with all the pictures.

ACTIVE LEARNING

Science – Recognizing cause and effect

Materials and preparation

- Set of paper strips (prepared by you before class starts)
- Set of pictures of places in town (prepared by you before class starts)

Before class, prepare a set of at least ten pictures of places in town. You can add to the set prepared for the previous class. Prepare the set of paper strips beforehand as well. Cut five paper strips and draw a clue about what people do in five of the places shown in your picture set. For example, draw a red cross or bottle of cough syrup if you have a drugstore among your places. Take a picture of a place (drugstore, for example). Show the picture to the students and ask, *What do we do in a drugstore?* Then show the paper strip related to the drugstore and give students some time to make a sentence: *We buy medicine and cosmetics in a drugstore.*

Set the two pieces – picture and paper strip – aside. Take another picture and ask, *What is a (place)?* Show the paper strip related to that place and encourage students to answer correctly: *A (supermarket) is a place where we go to (buy food).* Continue this procedure until you have worked with all the places in your bag, using the ones with a corresponding paper strip first. Help with vocabulary and grammar whenever needed. When you are finished, ask, *What is your favorite place in town? Why? What do you go there for?* and invite some volunteers to answer.

Engineering – Build your favorite place in town

Materials and preparation

- Colored and white envelopes – one for each student
- Glue
- Index cards – one for each student
- Building blocks and pieces or scrap materials – enough for students to build their favorite place in town
- Project Book page 63

Invite them to draw and color their favorite place in town. Instruct them to write the name of the place on top of the envelope. When they finish drawing, have them open their Project Book to page 63 and glue the envelope to the street illustration. While the glue dries, hand out Lego blocks and pieces or scrap materials for students to build their favorite place in town. Hand students index cards for them to write the name of the building and tape the index card to it.

DIFFERENTIATED INSTRUCTION

BELOW LEVEL
Sharing their favorite place in town

Materials and preparation

- Students' envelope building

In pairs, students share their favorite place in town and take turns saying sentences such as, *My favorite place in town is the bakery. A bakery is a place where we can buy bread, cookies, cakes, pastries, and pies.* Model before you assign the activity. Write the sentences on the board for students' reference. Walk around, monitor the activity, and help them as needed.

ABOVE LEVEL

In pairs, students share two of their favorite places in town and take turns saying sentences such as, *My favorite place in town is the bakery. A bakery is a place where we can buy bread, cookies, cakes, pastries, and pies.* Model before you assign the activity. Walk around, monitor the activity, and help them as needed.

CLOSING

Saying goodbye

Say *goodbye* to each student individually and ask them to say what their favorite part of the class was. Say, *See you tomorrow* and have them say it back to you.

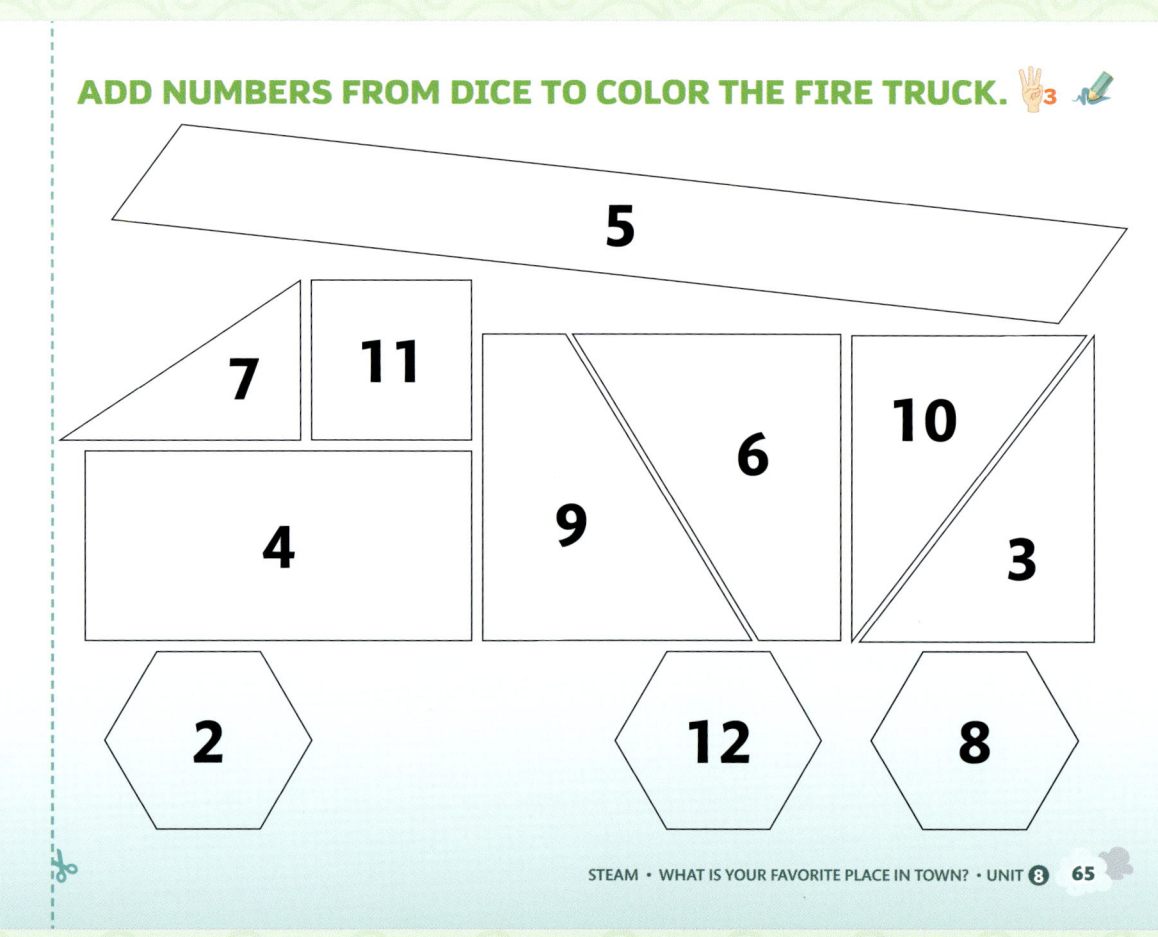

Learning goals
- Recognize the importance of different community workers
- Incorporate basic math skills into a game
- Build a climbing firefighter display

STEAM subjects
- Science
- Technology
- Engineering
- Arts
- Math

Thinking skills
Recognizing, classifying, sharing information

Main language content
Community workers
Fire truck, grow up
What do you want to be when you grow up?

OPENING

Circle time

Materials and preparation
- Visual schedule pictures

Say *hello* to students and invite them to sit in a circle. Show them the visual schedule pictures and explain what they are for. Say, *These pictures show our schedule for the day. Let's check them out!* Show all pictures, one at a time, and teach students the name of the subjects. Ask them to say what kind of things they may learn in these subjects and help them understand a little more about them.

> **Note to teachers**
> You can print out pictures of students doing these activities and use them for the visual schedule.

Science – Understanding the basic requirements for different jobs

Ask students, *What do you want to be when you grow up?* Explain the meaning of *grow up*, if necessary. Allow time for discussion and answers. Take a few of the most popular answers and write them on the board (make sure to include community helpers such as doctors, firefighters, and teachers). Then ask students, *What do you think you need in order to be a (teacher)?* Write down the keywords to their answers (for example, when a student says *I think you need a lot of patience*, write *patience* on the board). Help them with vocabulary. Continue until you have talked about all the occupations on the board.

ACTIVE LEARNING

Arts and math – Add numbers from dice to color the fire truck.

Materials and preparation
- Colored pencils or crayons
- Dice – two for each group of students
- Project Book page 65

Tell students to open their books to page 65 and elicit what they see. Go over the shapes, asking their names. Then explain that a fire truck is a vehicle that carries firefighters and equipment for fighting large fires, for example. Organize students into small groups and announce that you are going to play a math game with the fire truck illustration. Hand out a pair of dice to each group and explain that they will take turns rolling the dice, counting the dots in both, and coloring the corresponding shape on their fire truck. The dice should not be rolled a second time until everyone in the group is done coloring the first shape, and so on. Encourage them to help each other with the addition if one of them has trouble. You can turn this into a competition by having groups race against each other to be the first to complete their entire fire truck, or as you feel appropriate.

> **Note to teachers**
> This activity could be done more easily if students sit on the floor, so that the dice won't roll off of their desks.

Technology, engineering, and arts – Building a climbing firefighter display with a pulley system

Materials and preparation
- Cardboard strips (prepared by you before class starts)
- Colored pencils or crayons
- Teacher's Resources: Firefighter paper figue (one for each student)
- Glue or tape
- Scissors
- Straws
- String

Before class, print out a copy of the firefighter paper figure for each student. Also, cut cardboard into strips – each student should receive two 4 cm x 40 cm strips and five 4 cm x 10 cm strips. At the beginning of the lesson, explain that they are going to build a climbing firefighter display. Have a brief discussion about what firefighters do and why they are important to the community. Divide students into pairs. Hand students the firefighter figures and tell them to color them, having them relate the color of the uniform to the color of the firefighters' uniforms in their country. If you consider this a proper procedure, point out that every firefighter wears the same uniform to protect them from the dangers they face, so their little figure could be anybody, regardless of gender or any other factor. Once they have finished coloring, give them the other materials. Students should help each other attach the shorter cardboard strips to the longer ones to make the shape of a ladder, then attach two parallel straws to the back of the firefighter figure, using glue or tape. While they are doing this, cut pieces of string for each student, about a meter long, and distribute them. Have students thread the string through the straws, creating a loop at the top of the string (above the firefighter's head), and then tie each end of the string into a knot so that the figure won't fall off. Walk around the classroom giving assistance wherever needed. Once they are done, borrow a student's display or have your own already made to show them how it is done. Attach the ladder to the door of a cabinet or cupboard with tape. Then hang the firefighter figure from the knob by the string loop. Gently pull the strings one at a time and watch how the firefighter seems to climb the ladder. Encourage students to hang theirs up at home and show it to their families

DIFFERENTIATED INSTRUCTION

BELOW LEVEL
Science – Gathering and sharing personal information

In pairs, students ask each other questions about their families' occupations, such as *Who lives with you? What does your (mom) do?* Students then take turns asking and answering the questions. Model with a student first. Write the questions and the answers on the board for their reference.

ABOVE LEVEL

In pairs, students ask each other questions about their families' occupations, such as *Who lives with you? What does your (dad) do? Do they like it?* Students then take turns asking and answering the questions. Then have students choose one of their classmate's family members' jobs. Ask them again what they want to do when they grow up, but this time have them respond *I want to be a (job) like (classmate)'s (relative)* – for example, *I want to be a cook like Julia's mother*.

CLOSING

Saying goodbye

Say *goodbye* to each student individually and ask them to say what their favorite part of the class was. Say, *See you tomorrow!* and have them say it back to you.

IDENTIFY EACH WORKPLACE. STICK THE PROFESSIONAL WHO WORKS THERE.

STEAM • WHAT IS YOUR FAVORITE PLACE IN TOWN? • UNIT 8   67

Learning goals
- Recognize different occupations
- Role-play as a community worker
- Make a paper hat

STEAM subjects
- Science
- Arts
- Engineering

Thinking skills
Recalling, identifying, inferring, recognizing, describing, constructing

Main language content
Community workers

OPENING

Circle time

Materials and preparation
- Visual schedule pictures

Say *hello* to students and invite them to sit in a circle. Show them the visual schedule pictures and explain what they are for. Say, *These pictures show our schedule for the day. Let's check them out!* Show all pictures, one at a time, and teach students the name of the subjects. Ask them to say what kind of things they may learn in these subjects and help them understand a little more about them.

> **Note to teachers**
> Call on a student to be the class helper of the day. Tell this student to help you with materials and other simple tasks throughout today's lesson.

Science – Making deductions based on clues

Materials and preparation
- Sticky notes with professions (prepared by you before class starts)

Before class, prepare sticky notes with professions written on them – one profession on each note. You will need one sticky note for each student, but you can repeat professions if necessary. Students will have to describe the actions of the professionals, so choose the professions according to students' vocabulary skills. Organize students into pairs. Tell students that they are going to play a guessing game with professions. Explain that you will stick the name of a profession to the back of each student, and they cannot say the profession stuck on the back of their classmates. Give them an example. Ask a student to take one note and stick it to your back, but they cannot give you any clues. Ask a question about that profession for students to answer. Go on asking until you find out what professional you are. Explain that they have to give short, simple answers and they cannot use words that give up the other student's profession. Have the pairs of students stand up facing each other and then stick a note with a profession to the back of each student. The students look at their classmate's job. One student asks the first question and the other answers. Then it is the second student's turn. They go on like this, asking and answering questions, until one student from the pair finds out their profession. Walk around the class while students are working to offer help and ensure all students are playing the game. Here are some ideas on questions students can use. Add more questions to the list in order to give students enough options. If you consider it appropriate, you can write the questions on the board before the class starts.

Can I cook?
Do I carry books?
Do I have a secretary?
Do I travel for my job?
Do I wear a uniform?
Do I work in a hospital?
Do I work in a restaurant?
Do I work outside?
Do I work weekends?
Do I work with people?
Is my job dangerous?

ACTIVE LEARNING

Science – Identify each workplace. Stick the professional who works there.

Materials and preparation
- Project Book page 67
- Stickers

Lead students to their desks. Have them open their Project Book to page 67 and look at the pictures. Tell them to look at the first picture and ask, *What place is this?* Elicit answers from students. Teach the word *workplace*. Then ask, *Who works here?* Elicit from students again. Explain that they are going to use the stickers to complete the workplaces with the corresponding professionals. Tell them to look at all the pictures, decide where the first sticker goes, and only then peel it off and stick it to the correct place. When they finish this part of the activity, pair them up again. Tell them they are going to describe the professionals in the pictures to each other with complete sentences, such as, *He's a street cleaner. Street cleaners work on the streets. Street cleaners clean litter that accumulates on streets.* Each student will describe two of the professions presented in the pictures.

Engineering and arts – Making a hat to indicate your occupation and role-playing as different professionals

Materials and preparation
- Colored pencils
- Glue
- Teacher's Resources: Paper hats (one for each student) (prepared by you before class starts)
- Poster paper (one per student or have them share)
- Scissors

Before class, prepare paper hats for all the students. Get the templates of the paper hat at. On poster paper, draw one hat and some badges (police officer, firefighter, nurse, pilot). Prepare one sheet of poster paper for each student.

Tell students they are going to decide what professional they want to be today. Explain the badges so that they can decide. Tell them to color the badge they want and decorate the hat if they want to.

After they are done, instruct them on how to cut out their hat and glue the ends together to make it fit around their heads. Students then put their hats on and stand in front of the class all together. Decide in which order you will be calling them (alphabetical, by profession, or randomly) and have them introduce their job with its name and a simple fact about it. For example, *I am a doctor. I listen to people's hearts.* The students who have already introduced themselves go back to their desk. Continue until everyone has said their line.

Note to teachers
If students find it difficult to use glue for the hat, have them use tape instead.

DIFFERENTIATED INSTRUCTION

BELOW LEVEL
Arts – Role-playing as different community workers

Materials and preparation
- Students' paper hats

Students sit in a circle, each one holding the hat that they made. Explain to them that each time you clap your hands, they will pass their hat to the person on their right. Clap your hands a few times so that students can pass their hats around. Then have them look at the new hats they have and identify the job it represents. Choose a volunteer to name their new occupation. Repeat the process as many times as you feel necessary.

ABOVE LEVEL
Students sit in a circle, each one holding the hat that they made. Explain to them that each time you clap your hands, they will pass their hat to the person on their right. Clap your hands a few times so that students can pass their hats around. Then have them look at the new hats they have and identify the job it represents. Choose a volunteer to introduce themselves again, now with a new occupation and new facts about it. Repeat the process as many times as you feel necessary.

CLOSING

Saying goodbye

Materials and preparation
- Audio library - songs

Sing the *Goodbye song* (track 03) and invite students to sing along.

Notes

Notes

Notes

Notes

Notes

Notes

Notes

Notes

Notes